KEEPING PACE

KEEPING PACE

a grief journey measured in miles

Julie Fergus

Dedication

For every heart that has faced goodbye—
whether too soon or after a lifetime together.
May the road ahead bring you moments of light,
and the courage to keep going.

Prologue
The Weight of Flight

As winter gives way to spring, I dream of a hummingbird lying on the sidewalk, its small body torn open as a cat paws at it. The image wakes me with a jolt, its fragility heavy in my chest.

Earlier that day, on my lunch break, I had passed the hummingbird—tiny, iridescent, still. I nudged it off the pavement and covered it with a few leaves before walking on. But the dream wouldn't let me leave it there.

I return with a small box, lift the bird inside, and bring it home. In my front yard, just below Conor's upstairs window, I bury it, marking the place with a Mexican sage bush so hummingbirds can come and feed. Their wings flash in and out of the yard, and each time, I think of Papa.

He was always humming under his breath as he fixed what was broken. By the time Tom died, Papa had been gone more than a year. Still, I keep reaching for him—his presence, the way he cared by staying near.

The hummingbird becomes my way of holding on— proof that love, once given, lingers.

Even with that small comfort taking root outside my window, the ache keeps growing.

The Starting Line

The Loss

Chapter 1
Under Fluorescence

Tom's hand swallows mine as we sit across from the Emergency Room doctor. His palm is warm, a little damp, his grip firm enough to say *we're in this together.* We weren't hand-holders—not really—but tonight it feels necessary, a small act of solidarity as the doctor clicks through images on the monitor.

It's late. The fluorescent lights hum softly, washing the room in a pale glow. The sharp, medicinal bite of hand sanitizer lingers in the air, faint but insistent, and I wonder if I'll ever be able to smell it without remembering this night.

CT scans. A chest X-ray. Black-and-white shadows we don't yet understand.

My thumb grazes the edge of his silver wedding band, etched with Celtic spirals. We'd been married five years before he wore any ring at all—he didn't like the idea of being marked. Then one day in a small Celtic shop, he surprised me by slipping this one onto his finger. *I'd wear that,* he'd said.

Attempting to ground myself, I press my thumb to the cool metal as the doctor clears his throat. I hold on as if I can keep us anchored in the world we knew. Just hours earlier, I was heading upstairs for bedtime stories and toothbrushing when he called out from the living room. He gripped his opposite wrist and swung his arm to show me his limp hand. His eyes were wide, urgent. When he tried to speak, only a deep, guttural grunt came out. The left side of his face sagged, and the sound hollowed me out.

Something in my chest tightened. My hands shook as I reached for the keys.

Minutes blurred—the two of us in the car. On the way, I silently prayed that I didn't make the wrong decision to drive him instead of calling 911. The hospital doors slid open to bright light and the sharp scent of antiseptic. Nurses moved with quiet efficiency.

———

Three nights earlier, my brother Robert was staying with us. We were in the living room, the low hum of the dishwasher in the background, when I asked him if he was ever going to ask his girlfriend to marry him.

He shrugged, said his relationship wasn't perfect.

Tom leaned back in his chair, laughing loudly. "Do you think this is some magical, perfect relationship?" he said.

Robert just shrugged again.

Tom grinned and tossed a glance at me. "Your sister can really be a nag."

I hated that word. He was always telling me *nagging causes cancer*—not the disease itself, but the kind of slow rot that ate away at the ease of being together. I understood what he meant, but it still landed wrong. I meet his jab with a sweet smile that wasn't sweet at all.

Inside, it burned. I wanted to defend myself—to say that reminders aren't nagging, that keeping a family running takes effort—but the peacekeeper in me stayed quiet. I let it pass, at least on the surface.

"You just have to ask yourself if the good outweighs the bad," Tom said.

"And if you'd be better or worse off without her," I added.

The following night, I drove Tom to the Emergency Room (ER). His shoulder pain had been gnawing at him for over two weeks. His primary care physician had prescribed a muscle relaxant, but it hadn't helped. When I tried to massage the muscle, he flinched hard, like I'd hit a nerve. He was so desperate for relief, he'd started seeing a chiropractor.

At the ER, the staff directed their questions only at Tom, eyes fixed on him as if I wasn't there. Privacy rules. I leaned in, low enough for only him to hear. "Be sure to tell them your dad had a heart attack at forty-five," I said. Minutes later, they sent me to the waiting room to wait.

After an EKG and X-ray, the diagnosis was the same: pinched nerve. We were told to follow up with Tom's regular doctor.

The next day, Tom saw his chiropractor again before his appointment with his doctor.

"Your shoulder feels really abnormal," the chiropractor told him. "You should ask for a CT scan."

But Tom's doctor waved it off. "It's a pinched nerve. I'll refer you to physical therapy, but stop seeing the chiropractor —the manipulation could make it worse."

In the small exam room, the monitor glows in the dim light. Tom tightens his grip on my hand. The ER doctor clicks the mouse to display Tom's chest x-ray on the computer. His voice is steady, deliberate, but his words blur together. Something about scans, images, possibilities… then one word catches and holds: *lesion.*

I nod, though I don't fully understand.

Next, he clicks to the head CT, scrolling through the

layers. Gray and white matter slides past until he pauses. There—four dark patches. He points to the screen. I hear *lesion* again.

My eyes flick between the screen and his face, trying to make sense of it. I should be able to read these images, but because it's Tom's, my mind refuses to translate.

"I'm really sorry," he says finally, "but I think you have lung cancer that has spread to your brain. I suspect it's the reason for your shoulder pain and that it has likely already spread throughout your body."

The words land like a blow. The room feels too small, the air too thick. Tom's hand is still wrapped around mine, the edge of his wedding ring pressing into my skin, and I hold on tighter—as if pressure alone could keep us from being swept away.

Chapter 2
Monterey

Years earlier, on a trip to Monterey, the road ahead looked completely different.

The kids were away with friends. Tom was driving, one hand on the wheel, the other resting easily on the console. Out the window, the coast was alive—runners glided along the path, cyclists bent low over their handlebars, swimmers sliced through the cold, green-blue water. Farther out, surfers bobbed on their boards, waiting for the next big wave.

"I think I'd like to do a triathlon sometime," Tom said, eyes still on the road. "Do you think you'd want to do one?"

I let the question sit for a moment. "Maybe," I said finally, though my voice led on that I wasn't entirely sure.

The ocean past the point where I could stand had always unnerved me. When I was a girl, reaching for a seashell at the wrong time, a wave had pulled me under. I was tumbled so hard I didn't know which way was up, and when I swam for what I thought was the surface, I hit the ocean floor instead. By the time I broke through for air, I was gasping, disoriented, and wandered down the beach in tears, unable to find the towel where my dad was waiting.

I didn't say no to the triathlon because I didn't want to

disappoint him. I figured I could work up the courage—ease into the idea, maybe start with a pool or a lake. A few years later, we'd go on to do a few triathlons together, though never ones with ocean swims.

That day in Monterey, the sea looked calmer. We spent the morning sipping cappuccinos in a small café, wandering the shops on Cannery Row, and walking the path that traced the water's edge. The air was cool enough for a sweater, but the sun shone steady. At one point we stopped at a bench and simply sat, letting the quiet soak in. I loved this about us; we could have moments of stillness without feeling the need to fill the silence.

"I would like to do a triathlon someday," I said, "but first, I'd like to run a marathon."

Tom turned toward me, a small, knowing smile breaking across his face. "I want to run a marathon too. Let's pick one in the next year."

The rest of the drive home was all talk of marathons. Big Sur—maybe someday. The cities we might travel to. The training plans we'd need to follow. He told me to take the lead in researching, his voice light with excitement, as if we'd just mapped out a new adventure neither of us could yet imagine.

Within days, we'd decided: the Napa Valley Marathon, March 2002. We marked it on the calendar, our first start line in sight.

Chapter 3
Between Beeps

Tom is admitted to the hospital—the same hospital where my stepfather, Jim, whom we called Papa B, had his cancer treatments a little over a year earlier. Although the chemotherapy and other treatment had cured Papa's cancer, I still felt dread from being here again. The fact that Papa had a heart attack and died just days after being told he was cancer-free did not give me confidence.

Tom has a series of tests done.

We wait. Hours stretch and fold in on themselves. I watch the door, willing someone to come in and say something—anything.

When the scans finally come back, the scans begin to tell a familiar story—lesions are scattered throughout his body, in the same places he's complained about over the years.

The doctor comes in with the latest results, a chart tucked under his arm.

"As we suspected, there are lesions throughout your body, Mr. Fergus," he says.

He pauses, glancing between the two of us, as if gauging how much more to say.

Tom waits.

"Your hip. Your back. Your shin."

"And the shoulder?" Tom asks.

"The shoulder doesn't show anything."

Tom lets out a small laugh. "I know you're telling me I've got lesions everywhere else," he says, "but what is going on with my shoulder? That's what's killing me."

The doctor's eyes flick to me, then back to Tom. He hesitates, searching for a response that doesn't quite come.

Tom doesn't press. He just sits there, one hand resting on the tray table, waiting.

The doctor says he'll have the radiologist take another look. Then he's gone.

We let the information settle between us, conversation giving way to quiet.

When Tom's primary physician comes to visit him in the hospital, I step outside. I can't bear to look at him.

The fresh air is sharp against my lungs, but my thoughts are anything but clear. I'm angry that the lesions were missed. Angry with myself, too, though I don't know where to place the blame.

Tom had always had a high pain tolerance—the shoulder, the hip, the back—he'd brushed it all off as overuse, as weight, as nothing urgent. The only moment that ever unsettled me was that curtain of vision loss years earlier. Just adding a statin never felt like enough, but I told myself he was in good hands.

Tom, however, isn't angry at all. Later, he tells me he *likes the guy* and that anyone could have missed it.

I call my friend Liz, a nurse practitioner I've known since our days in the pediatric ICU. I tell her about the visual curtain—how five years earlier, half Tom's field of vision went dark for several minutes and then returned.

"Did they image him?" she asks.

"No," I say. "They said it was probably cholesterol."

"Julie," she says carefully, "something like that would typically warrant a CT scan."

There's no rewinding the clock. We can only keep moving forward, test by test.

Everything is under examination—his brain, his shoulder, his lungs—each test pointing in a different direction. The door to Tom's hospital room never seems to close as various teams come in one by one.

The next day, an **MRI** of his shoulder reveals the culprit. Unlike the other lesions, this one has eaten away the bone in his shoulder blade, leaving holes and divots like Swiss cheese. Similar punch-like holes are visible in the bone of his upper arm. No wonder the chiropractor thought it felt strange.

When the pulmonologist comes by later, he explains that "brain cancer is happy to stay in the brain, but lung cancer is known to venture elsewhere," and that without a biopsy, they can't yet call the lesions tumors.

On the second day of his hospital stay, they try to get the confirmation we need, but the swelling and damage in Tom's lungs make it impossible to collect a clear sample. Instead, they pass a tiny brush through a bronchoscope deep into the lung, gently scraping cells from the airways. Those cells are cultured, a process that takes days before results come back.

In the meantime, the back-and-forth between home and the hospital wears on me. A pattern emerges—drop the boys at school, drive straight to the hospital, listen to the doctors, translate what Tom can't take in. Between rounds, I check work emails on my BlackBerry, send family updates, try to keep the rest of life from unraveling. Some days I stay a little later; others I rush home and circle back again before visiting hours end.

I still have no real sense of what I'm in for. The days are already blurring together, and I know I can't manage it all alone. I begin reaching out—to neighbors, the boys' baseball Team Moms, and family. Help comes quickly. The boys have rides home, neighbors offer to watch and feed them, and my sister Carol swings by with groceries and casserole dishes full of ready-made meals.

While the support at home steadies me, the reality at the hospital remains unchanged. Without an official diagnosis, they can't give us a prognosis or talk about treatment. Over the next several days, Tom endures an exhausting battery of tests—scans, scopes, lab work, and even a procedure to drain fluid from his lung to help him breathe more easily. Still, we leave the hospital without answers. The doctors mention possibilities like tuberculosis or a fungal infection, but with so much pointing toward cancer, hope feels hard to reach.

"How much time do you think I have left?" Tom asks me.

"My best guess is somewhere between three and six months," I tell him.

I don't explain how I know—how many charts I've read, how many families I've seen face the same impossible question. It's a calculation that lives somewhere between data and intuition, a nurse's instinct honed over years of watching bodies fail.

But saying it to my own husband feels different, like I'm pronouncing a sentence I'd do anything to take back.

———

When we get home from the hospital, Tom wants to sleep in the comfort of our own bed. Upstairs, we curl up in each other's arms. I lie beside him, feeling helpless, as tears stream down my face. The man I have built my life with is dying and there isn't anything I can do. Tom pulls me to his chest as I sob. Then he lifts my head up and looks at me with his beautiful blue eyes.

"I love you, Julie," he says, kissing me.

The words are rare, which makes them all the more precious.

From the beginning of our relationship, Tom had told me he didn't want me to *need* his reassurance to know I was beautiful or loved. He wanted me to believe in myself, to carry that strength whether he said it or not. And while I always knew he loved me, moments like this—his voice whispering the words into the quiet, and his arms around me—feel like treasures I will hold on to for a long time.

He is weak, but we manage to make love to each other—a moment I will revisit often in the years ahead.

In the days that follow, we move gently through the hours, holding on to each other.

We tell the boys only what we know—that tests were run, and the doctors are still figuring things out. I can see the worry in both of their eyes, the way they keep glancing between us, searching for reassurance. We promise to share more when we can, but the truth is, we're still bracing for it ourselves.

Tom calls Dylan to explain what's happening. Dylan is twenty-seven, Tom's son from his first marriage, and by that evening, he's already on the road, driving north from West Hollywood to be with us. Having him close again feels both comforting and sobering—like the circle of our family is tightening, preparing for whatever comes next.

Four days later, we return to the hospital for the results. The lung specialist confirms that Tom indeed has cancer and ushers us to meet with an oncologist. I open my notebook, write down every word as he speaks, making sure I don't miss a thing.

"It's metastatic, or stage 4, non-small cell lung cancer. It is so widespread that there aren't any treatment options available," he tells us.

We have the option to start palliative radiation along with steroids to, hopefully, make the final time a little better.

"Either way," the oncologist says, "you have about a year left."

"One year!" Tom says, a little relieved that it won't be as quick as we'd feared. The words stay with us as we leave the cool, sterile office into the late-afternoon sun.

Tom moves slowly, worn out from the day. That evening, we know we can't put it off any longer.

We sit down with Conor and Ryan to explain what is going on. Conor is fourteen—tall for his age, the kind of tall that makes strangers expect more from him—and Ryan is eight, still small enough to lean into his brother without thinking. Less than a year and a half ago, they lost their grandfather Papa B to a heart attack just days after he'd been told he was cancer-free. Not wanting to sugarcoat the news, Tom was very honest with the boys.

"There are four tumors in my brain and one of them caused the stroke you saw," Tom explains.

"But you can get better. Right?" Ryan asks as he tries not to cry.

"The cancer is all over my body, in my lungs and bones, and there isn't any medicine strong enough to make it better."

Conor puts his arm around Ryan, as Ryan begins crying.

"The doctor told us that I won't die for about a year," Tom continues, "It is only a year, but I am going to do some radiation treatments so that we can make the best of the time we have left."

He motions the boys over and hugs them while they cry.

Chapter 4
The Weight of Becoming

Ryan and I head upstairs to get ready for bed. Conor lingers. Fourteen is such a precarious age—too old to cry openly, too young to carry anything heavy.

Tom lifts his hand—not beckoning, just a small, familiar gesture that means *come sit with me.*

"Hey, buddy," he says. "Come here for a second."

Conor settles on the far end of the couch, posture tight, jaw pulsing the way it does when he's trying not to break. Tom shifts a little closer, reaching for his hand. His grip is weaker now, but the intention is unmistakable.

"I don't know how this next year is going to unfold," Tom says quietly. "I'm going to need your help to support your brother and mom."

Conor doesn't answer—he just nods once, eyes fixed on his hands.

Tom takes a breath, wanting to get this right.

"Conor," he says gently, "you're the man of the house now."

The words land differently this time. When the kids were younger and Tom left for a trip, he used to say it with pride—

You get to be the man of the house while I'm gone—a way to lift him up, to make him feel strong.

But this moment isn't that.

Not even close.

Conor inhales sharply, as if trying to grow into a responsibility that's suddenly much heavier. His chin lifts a fraction. He nods too quickly—brave, scared, determined, all at once.

Tom squeezes his hand again. "Take care of Ryan," he adds. "He's going to need your support. And your mom too."

Another nod, slower this time. His throat moves with a swallow that sticks halfway down. Tom places a hand between his shoulder blades—steady, reassuring, the way only a father can.

After a long moment, Conor stands and slips upstairs. His footfalls are quiet on the staircase. He steps into Ryan's room just as I'm settling in beside Ryan for story time. He pulls out another book and climbs onto the bed next to his brother.

In the NICU, steady beeping filled the room as Conor walked in holding Tom's hand, his eyes widening as he passed the rows of tiny swaddled babies. A couple of hours after birth, Ryan had turned blue, showing signs of respiratory distress, and now faced a week-long stay for IV antibiotics. At over eight pounds, he was two to three times larger than the others.

At six years old, Conor was thrilled to meet Ryan. He'd watched his friends welcome new siblings with envy. His big brother, Dylan, had left for college on the East Coast just two weeks earlier.

I knew this world—the monitors, the lines, the rhythm of care. Years in the PICU had trained me to read every alarm, every nurse's glance. The medical part didn't scare me; I understood it. What unnerved me was the other part—the helplessness of being on the parent side of it.

The nurses helped Conor into a recliner, where he seemed almost as small as the babies around him. Tom gently lifted Ryan from my arms and placed him in Conor's. I hovered close, the nurse watching the transfer, the mother taking it in. Tom leaned close and told Conor he could slip his finger into the indentation of Ryan's pacifier to feel him sucking. Conor tried it, his face softening as he looked over at me and smiled —a smile that felt like the first thread of a lifelong connection. The hum of equipment faded into the background, and for a moment, it was just the three of them in their own quiet world.

After a day in the NICU, Ryan transferred to a level II nursery—still under the same close monitoring but with less intensive nursing care. By then, I had been discharged and was going home at night, leaving him in the care of the nurses. Professionally, I trusted them completely. Personally, it gutted me to walk out of the hospital without my baby. Knowing too much didn't make it easier—it only sharpened the edges of what could go wrong.

At the end of the week, just minutes after his final dose of antibiotics—an injection after his IV gave out—Conor and I wheeled him out of the hospital. Buckled into his car seat and tucked into a wagon with his hospital things, he cried the whole way down the hall. Conor had been waiting all week for this moment, and now Ryan's lusty wail, so loud and certain, was more than just proof his lungs were clear—it was the sound of relief, of release, of finally going home.

A week later, Tom's mom came to stay with us. I used her visit as an opportunity to spend more time with Conor, making sure he didn't feel left out. But he acted out toward Grandma Fergus. The more he did, the more I had her take care of Ryan so I could focus on him.

The night before she left, I told Conor that once she was gone, I would have less time with him because of the baby. I asked why he was being so mean to her. His face crumpled, and tears filled his eyes as he whispered that Grandma was hogging our baby. He wanted her to know Ryan was ours. I pulled him into my lap, holding him as his small shoulders shook.

Those same tears pool in his eyes as he takes in the news that their dad is dying. The boys are older now, but that protective streak—that fierce sense of *ours*—is still there.

Chapter 5
Full Moon

The Pacific stretched out before us, black and endless, broken only by the white shimmer of moonlight riding the waves. Halfway down the beach, a bonfire flickered, voices drifting faintly on the wind. At the far end, jagged rocks guarded the mouth of a tunnel that leads to more beach on the other side. People waded through the water to reach it, but we stayed put, content to just sit in the quiet.

The moon was full, and I loved it. It felt like borrowed daylight, soft but steady, lighting the world when everything else had gone dark. Even as a kid, I'd search for it, tracing its slow rhythm through the sky—the sliver, the half, the slow return to roundness. I didn't understand it then, only that its light made the night feel less lonely. The full moon didn't demand attention; it simply shone.

Tom brought a small blanket and draped it around my shoulders. He wore only his worn black jean jacket, shoulders squared against the chill. His arm around me was solid and sure, and the closeness sent a ripple of warmth through me that had nothing to do with the blanket.

We didn't talk much. I listened to the rhythm of the waves and to the sound of my own pulse quickening. I was still in the stage where just being near him made my stomach flutter. He was eight years older, divorced, with a young son, and he carried a kind of wisdom I couldn't yet match.

No one ever taught me how to feel sure of myself. I've spent most of my life trying to earn words like proud or love. Somehow he doesn't see me the way I see myself. When he looks at me, it's as if he sees more—someone I haven't quite become yet.

Chapter 6
Putting Things in Order

When Tom is discharged from the hospital, the social worker leaves us with a stack of forms. Buried among them is an Advance Health Care Directive. We sit on the couch, talk through Tom's wishes, check the boxes, and ask a neighbor to come over and witness his signature.

Tom is still himself—mostly. The words sometimes come out wrong. His body occasionally lags behind his intentions. But he is alert, present, and doing his best to absorb what is happening.

He sends emails and makes phone calls to close friends and family. He updates his employer and completes the paperwork they need.

He and his good friend Ed, whom he worked with for years and even lived with when we first started dating, go out for lunch. He needs to tell Ed in person. They are gone for a couple of hours. When they return, Ed comes over and pulls me into a long hug.

"Julie," Ed says, forcing a smile.

Still in his arms, I start to cry.

"Let it go," he urges. I hear the strain beneath his usual optimism.

In the days that follow, there is a steadiness to it all—not denial, not calm exactly, but momentum. As if keeping things in motion might hold the fear at bay.

Knowing we have a year is only somewhat reassuring. We don't know how difficult the year ahead will be. There have already been moments that remind us that the coming year might not be so easy.

"We need to go go-la-blah," Tom blurts.

I watch the surprise register on his face.

"Did you hear that?" he asks.

"I did."

He tries again but it still comes out wrong.

We look at each other. He grabs his laptop, launches the email program, and types out "We need to go to the bank."

He turns the screen toward me.

I nod.

At the bank, we add my name to Tom's banking accounts so that I can easily access the money to pay bills in the coming year.

———

When we get home, the house is quiet. Everything that needed signing has been signed. Tom's sister, Kathy, is already there.

Tom suggests I go for a run.

They plan to sit together in the courtyard out front for a bit before coming inside. He says it casually, but I know he can feel that I need a release. I also think he wants a few minutes alone with Kathy.

I choose to stay close, and keep the run short. Nothing ambitious. I tell myself I'll be gone fifteen minutes.

The air feels tight from the start. Not cold, not hot—just

heavy. I make it less than a quarter mile before my throat starts to close. It's sudden and sharp, like my body has decided to stop cooperating. I can't get a full breath. Each inhale feels shallow, panicked. I slow, then stop, bent forward with my hands on my knees, gasping.

For a moment, I think I'm going to pass out.

And then, just as clearly, I think: *Tom is dying. And I'm not there.*

The thought lands fully formed, no logic attached. Just certainty. The kind that doesn't ask permission.

I turn around immediately.

I don't run so much as lurch back toward the house, my chest burning, my vision narrowing. The distance feels longer than it is. I'm not even a quarter mile away, but it might as well be miles.

When I reach the house, I look through the window first. I see him sitting there, still upright, still breathing. Talking.

I'm relieved he's still there and terrified of the moment he won't be.

That's when it hits.

I start sobbing so hard I can barely walk. The sound of it surprises me—raw, animal, louder than I expect. I can't bring myself to go inside like that. I don't want him to see me unravel.

So I sit down on the curb instead.

I let it come—all of it. The gasping, the shaking, the certainty of it—Tom is dying.

I don't know how long I sit there. Eventually the sobbing slows. My breathing evens out. The house stays quiet. He's still inside.

When I finally stand and wipe my face, I know something has shifted. I don't have language for it yet. I only know this: Running isn't taking me away from the fear anymore. It's carrying me straight into it.

Chapter 7
The Year Collapses

Tom begins radiation right away. The process of mapping exact target areas is extensive, the technology precise and exacting. In addition to the radiation, Tom is prescribed an oral steroid that reduces the swelling in his brain caused by the tumors but also reduces the swelling and lessens the side effects of the treatments.

The improvements are immediate. Tom can now engage in longer, more coherent conversations with us. His balance has also improved, enabling him to move around more effectively.

However, these positive changes are temporary.

Tom is scheduled for his third radiation treatment, but he is so unsteady this morning that he can't keep anything down and cannot walk. Although I haven't personally witnessed it, I have a hunch that he might have had another stroke.

I promptly call the Cancer Treatment Center and am advised to skip the scheduled treatment and return to the ER for intravenous steroids and hydration.

Tom's brother, Joe, arrives just in time to help me get him

into the car. Together, we steady him, each holding an arm, and guide him to the passenger seat.

By this time, it is clear that Tom is having more strokes. It is a vicious cycle: tumors cause swelling, swelling causes strokes, and the strokes cause more swelling. From how rapidly things are changing, it is doubtful that we'll even have the three months we once believed. We certainly are not going to have a year with him.

My gut feeling tells me that the progression of Tom's symptoms doesn't match the prognosis we'd been given. A repeat CT confirms that he is continuing to have more and more strokes. He is now having difficulty conveying his needs and asking questions, so I am allowed to advocate for him.

"The way he is deteriorating does not align with the 1 year prognosis we've been given," I say, sure that we haven't been told everything. I insist that the oncologist be called.

"What did Hospice tell you?" the ER physician asks.

"Hospice?" I say, "Hospice is for patients with less than six months to live. Tom has a year!"

The ER doctor rifles through Tom's chart again, "Hospice orders were written prior to his discharge."

Now, I am fuming. The hospitalists insisted they didn't know it was cancer when Tom was discharged. The ER doctor excuses herself and leaves to call the oncologist. When she returns she can hardly make eye contact with us.

"Unfortunately, the doctor can't come in," she says. "We reviewed your case. I'm so sorry—but it is only a matter of time before death." Tom's eyes well up.

"How long?" I ask.

"Weeks. Possibly days," she said.

"Mr. Fergus, we would like you to stay overnight for hydration and IV steroids while the referral to hospice gets put in place."

She continues, "I am really sorry that this was not initiated before."

Joe and I remain at the hospital until late. By the time we leave, Tom is still in the ER waiting for a bed to open up in the main hospital.

In the meantime, Ryan went home from school with a neighbor whose sons play with our boys. Later, after getting a ride home from baseball practice, Conor joins him. They do their homework and eat dinner with the neighbors before returning home to wait for us. With Tom still waiting for a bed to free up on the floor, Joe and I go home to get some rest and update the boys.

The following morning, I am met by the charge nurse in the hallway.

"Your husband was quite disoriented last night. He kept trying to get out of bed and pulled out his IV. We moved him across from the nurses' station so we can keep an eye on him, and the bed will alarm if he tries to get up. He is restrained right now, but we can remove the restraints as long as you are with him."

"Disoriented?" I say angrily. "He's not disoriented; he's ANGRY!"

I storm into the room where Tom is tied to the bed, like a combative drug addict, with four leather restraints.

"We need to get him out of here. This is not how he would want to die," I tell Joe.

Chapter 8
The Season Turns

The hospice intake visit is scheduled before we leave the hospital. I insist on a hospital bed and rattle off every reason I can: he'll need his head elevated to breathe, and our bedrooms are all upstairs.

We arrive home to discover that Dylan has already transformed the family room into a warm, private space for Tom. Curtains hang over the sliding glass door and hallway entry. The loveseat has been pushed aside to make room for the bed. A fire burns in the fireplace, taking the last edge off the winter chill.

Hospice sets us up with weekly visits from a nurse, a home health aide for bathing, and a social worker.

The nurse arrives first. She walks through the house with us, taking in the bed Dylan has set up, the cleared space, the bathroom just steps away. I tell her all the bedrooms are upstairs. She nods, approving.

"Good call on the hospital bed," she says.

"Who will be the primary caregiver?" she asks.

Tom points at me.

"That would be me," I say. "I'm a nurse. I used to do

home health and palliative care—mostly pediatrics. Family will help with the boys."

She doesn't ask for more.

We sit with Tom and talk about pain. That's the main thing, I tell her—keeping him comfortable. She explains the morphine that can be given under his tongue, the Ativan for anxiety or sleep.

"I'm not really anxious," Tom says.

She smiles gently. "It helps in more ways than one. We'll have it, just in case."

He nods.

By the time she leaves, everything has a place. We do too.

With that settled, the rest of the world begins to organize itself around us.

Tom has six siblings and agrees to see them—but only one at a time. His family helps with the boys—rides to school and baseball, swim lessons—while I care for Tom.

The social worker talks to each of the boys about what to expect and makes plans to bring supplies so they can take an imprint of Tom's hand to keep with them.

Though they help with the boys, his siblings worry about Tom's care and press for more support. I find a small notepad on the counter, already filled—agency names, phone numbers, hourly rates written in careful block letters. Someone has done the research.

I stand there longer than I mean to, the pen marks blurring as my eyes move back and forth across the page. Then I close the pad, carry it upstairs, and slide it into a drawer.

His youngest sister, Mary, watches me for a while before she asks, "Why don't you just sit by his bedside and read?"

The question is gentle. Reasonable.

It still hits me.

I shrug, because anything else would spill out too fast.

I can't tell her that sitting feels like abandonment. That

every minute I'm not watching his breathing, his color, the way his hand curls feels like negligence instead of love. That I'm already carrying the weight of missing this once.

———

Now the disease moves fast. He's having one or two mini-strokes a day. The boys spend time with him after school.

I take photos of each of them with their dad, knowing they may never want to look at them, but keep them anyway.

"I don't know if they'll ever want these," I say to Tom, lifting the camera. "But I want to take them."

Before this, the last picture I had of him was at our favorite Mexican restaurant. Ryan had my PalmPilot and was snapping photos of everyone. Tom hated being photographed, but he let him. He smirked and lifted his middle finger to the lens—defiant, playful. We had no idea it would be the last photo before the stroke.

He nods and reaches for the remote, lifting the head of the bed a little higher.

I call the boys in.

"Sit by your dad for a second," I say, keeping my voice light.

One at a time, they perch on the edge of the bed beside him. I take the photos quickly, not wanting to stretch the moment any longer.

I want one with him too.

I don't ask.

One afternoon, after school, Conor comes into the room and sits beside his dad. He's wearing his baseball cap, brim bent just the way he likes it. After a moment, he slips it off and turns it over in his hands before looking up.

"Some of the guys on my team," he says, "they have Bible verses written inside their hats. Like, under the brim."

Tom nods, watching him carefully.

"They say it gives them courage," Conor adds. "Helps them believe in themselves."

He hesitates, then holds the cap out. "Will you pick one for me? Write it in here?"

Tom takes the hat and turns it slowly, as if orienting himself. He studies the inside of the brim for a long time—longer than feels comfortable. His brow furrows. I can see the effort it takes to hold the thought, to will his hand to obey.

Conor waits, quiet, hopeful.

Tom finally uncaps the marker. His hand moves awkwardly, the letters coming out uneven, shaky. When he's done, there's only a wavering line of ink where a verse should be.

Conor takes the hat back and looks at it. His face doesn't change, but his shoulders round forward, his head dipping as if to protect something inside him. He pulls the cap on and walks out of the room without saying anything.

Years earlier, in our old little house in Cupertino, Tom and Conor turned the empty lot next door into a practice pitching mound. With Ryan "helping," they measured the space between mound and plate. Tom crouched to catch, as Conor pitched. Before long, Conor was throwing hard enough that a cup became mandatory.

That was before.

I go to check on Conor.

———

One night after dinner, Ryan helps his aunt put cookie dough on the baking sheet, sneaking one into his mouth when she isn't looking. When the cookies come out, I blow on one and hand it to Tom, who is sitting with us in the living room. He takes a bite and closes his eyes as if to savor the taste.

"Mmm, mmm, mmm…" he moans.

A soft ripple of laughter moves through the room—not loud or carefree, but warm and fleeting. The kind you cling to because you don't know how many more will come.

Chapter 9
By the Fireplace

By morning, the decline is unmistakable.

Tom limps down the hallway, dragging his leg, urine soaking through his sweatpants. He's banging into the walls as he goes, determined to go on his own.

I see Conor as he bolts out the door, not wanting to see his dad like this. I want to follow him, but I have to stop Tom from climbing the stairs. Through the window, I see Conor on the bench out front, sobbing and pounding his fists. When I go out a few minutes later, he's gone.

Later that day, Tom is sitting in the family room by the fireplace. Bob Dylan's *Modern Times* is playing, the same album he's had on repeat these days, like Tom always did when he had a new album. The fire is low and quiet. For a moment, he looks almost settled.

When he goes to stand and head for the bathroom, it happens all at once. His legs simply give way beneath him. I grab his arm as he goes down, but I can't slow him. He drops back hard into the chair, the impact splintering the frame.

Wood cracks. Cushions collapse. The chair gives out completely.

This time is different. Tom can't get up.

I call for help. One of his brothers is on the way. While I wait, I pull a pillow from the bed and slide it under his head. I lay a blanket over him. He's still, his breathing shallow. I curl up beside him on the floor and cry quietly, careful not to make it worse.

It takes four of us to lift him safely.

I keep thinking I should have done something sooner. Held him better. Stopped him. Not let him fall.

When we finally get him into bed, he doesn't get up again.

From here on, everything narrows. He's confined to the bed. Diapers replace trips to the bathroom. Words disappear. Eating is gone too. The losses come all at once, revealing themselves one by one.

I can feel the end approaching, even if I don't yet understand how close it is.

Chapter 10
What We Held Onto

When Tom and I first started dating, he didn't even own a TV. He and Dylan shared quiet evenings —eating together, talking about their days, and reading books. Tom was pursuing his master's degree in English Literature, and they lived in a tiny house downtown. Bedtime was its own ceremony.

Tom read all sorts of stories to Dylan, but when I watched him read *Winnie the Pooh*—seeing the tenderness between father and son—that made me realize I was falling in love with him. Tom brought the story new life, giving each character a distinct voice: Pooh was gentle and sincere, Piglet nervous and fluttery, Tigger booming with enthusiasm, Kanga motherly, and Roo bursting with excitement.

When the book was finished, Dylan giggled beneath his blankets, as Tom smoothed the sheets, tucked the covers snugly around him, pressed a kiss to his forehead, and turned out the light.

They only watched television when visiting Tom's parents or Ed.

That all changed when *Twin Peaks* was about to premiere. He went out and bought a TV and a VCR. Tom admired the director and didn't want to miss what promised to be something different.

Years later, *American Dreams* became our thing. Sunday nights belonged to it. The kids enjoyed it, but even if they hadn't, Tom would have made them sit with us. It was music, culture, a history lesson, and family time all in one. If people happened to be visiting when it came on, they were expected to stay and watch—quietly. We scheduled our life around it.

Sometimes Tom saved his ironing for *American Dreams* nights. He'd set up the ironing board in the opening between the living room, where the TV sat, and the dining room table. He'd press his shirts and slacks during the commercials and the Bandstand scenes, then leave the iron still plugged in and slip into the living room to watch the more intense moments with us.

When the show ended, the kids might ask a question or two, and Tom would explain the moment's significance—why it mattered, what it meant in the bigger picture. He always made sure they understood not just the story, but the history woven into it.

Chapter 11
The Final Days

I t's been only twenty days since his first stroke, but it feels like forever. When I finally admit I can't do this alone, I reach out to our meditation community. The men's group takes turns sitting by Tom's bedside at night so I can rest. They might meditate, read, doze in the chair, or give him his pain or anxiety medicine when he needs it.

Tonight, it's Tom's friend David who arrives after dinner and spends a couple of hours with us before we head upstairs. Ryan plays Old Maid with him by the fire while Conor does homework on the loveseat.

After, we leave Tom in David's care and go up to bed. I tuck both boys in, spending extra minutes with each of them —something I haven't had the luxury of doing in weeks.

The following morning, after four glorious hours of sleep, I awaken to the sound of Tom's moans coming through the heater vent. I stay in bed, listening for thirty more minutes, hoping the moaning will stop. But it doesn't and, they sound more urgent—like cries for help.

Downstairs, David gives me a quick report before leaving for home. As I go to give Tom a dose of morphine, I see the remains of the last dose pooling in his mouth. I try to soak it up with a tissue before squirting the next dose under his tongue. The morphine under Tom's tongue isn't absorbing. He's still in so much pain.

I call hospice to ask about switching delivery method from oral to a subcutaneous infusion—placing a small needle under the skin. A small pump delivers a steady infusion of morphine without the need for an IV.

It will take time to get the doctor's order, prepare the medicine, and send a nurse to set it up. While I wait, I hold Tom's hand.

"I'm sorry you're hurting, Tom. I've called for stronger pain meds."

Several hours pass before I call again. The kids have now left for school and Tom's sister, Kathy is here to help out and be with Tom.

"Everyone is in a meeting," the receptionist tells me.

I look at the hospice magnet on our fridge: *24-Hour Service.*

"You run a hospice," I say, trying to stay calm.

"You provide a 24-hour service. My husband is dying. If you can tell me the pharmacy has the order and is mixing it, I'll wait for the meeting to end. If not, I need to talk to someone now."

I'm put on hold. A nurse comes on the line.

"I don't know what happened—there's no record of your call. I'll contact the pharmacy immediately."

She suggests giving Tom Ativan with the morphine to help absorption. I do, then climb into bed beside him. Tears soak the sheet.

"It's okay to go now, Tom. I promise I'll take care of Conor and Ryan. I love you. We'll be okay."

Not long after, the moaning stops. His breaths grow shallow, barely lifting his chest, and his skin feels cool under my hand.

The phone rings. It's the hospice nurse.

"It will take time to prepare the infusion. I'm going to pick up a morphine injection to hold him over."

"Don't bother," I say. "You won't make it on time."

Kathy, just outside the room, hears me. She grips the wall and crumbles in tears.

"I want to give you a hug," I tell her, "but I can't leave him. Come here, Kathy. I promise it won't be any worse."

She steps to his side, and I wrap one arm around her while holding Tom's hand with the other. Together, we watch a single tear roll down his cheek as he takes his final breath.

Chapter 12
Celebration of Life

Almost immediately, questions turn to the service. I'm not ready to think about it, but they're here now—his older brother, Mike, has come from Hawaii; his younger brother, Joe, from New York. Others are already in the air or arranging to come.

"You need to do it now," Mike says.

I'm not ready. Arranging Tom's funeral makes it real.

I think of my boys—how they will sit through this, how they will try to understand it. I remember trying to understand once, too.

I'm sitting in a church pew beside my siblings at my grandfather's funeral, tears streaming as we try to stay still.

My youngest sister, Carol, too young to understand, whispered, "Why is Grandpa in a suitcase?"

My brother pulled her close: "He's taking a trip to heaven."

We break into giggles until my mom's sharp pinch stops us.

Like me, Tom was raised Catholic but hadn't practiced in adulthood. He wanted the boys to choose their own beliefs, so we hadn't raised them in the faith. His death came so quickly, we never discussed what he wanted for his celebration of life. Still, I remember him joking at his father's funeral about combining a Catholic Mass with his meditation community. It had been a joke—but one with a hint of seriousness.

Initially, I considered holding a Catholic Mass now and a memorial later, but I decided instead to follow Tom's "instructions" in a single celebration.

At his mom's funeral, rows of priests and nuns filled the church, Tom said, "Your Uncle Randy will be a Cardinal by the time I die. If he does my Mass, I'll have bragging rights with Mom and Dad in heaven."

Uncle Randy—Bishop of Reno—had always had mutual respect for Tom. I could hear Tom's voice teasing as I dialed. I told him about the stroke, the cancer, the death that came eleven months too soon.

"I'm so sorry, Julie. How can I help?" he asked.

"We were able to secure a church, but their priest isn't available. Would you be able to do the Mass for Tom?"

"Yes," he said after checking his calendar. "I can't stay long afterward, but I'll be there."

Plans took shape quickly. Joe arranged the cremation. Tom's sister Judy, a nun, booked the church and helped me choose songs and readings. My dad offered to print the programs, my sister Carol asked a friend of hers to create a slideshow.

As we sorted through boxes and albums, I was frustrated by how few photos I had of Tom. He hated having his picture taken. The last one—taken days before his stroke—showed him scowling and flipping off the camera.

Judy pulled out a photo of herself in her habit with Tom and their mom, then launched into a favorite story: how little Tom, curious about the habit, once peeked through her door again and again until she shooed him away. The next morning, he found the headdress on her dresser, slipped it on, and walked into the kitchen where his mom was preparing to cook breakfast. As Judy retells the story we've heard numerous times over the years, I remember Tom sharing a very entertaining version of the story for her fiftieth Jubilee celebration. "She wants to hit me. She wants to laugh. She has a frying pan in her hand..." Tom told this story, complete with sound effects that brought the whole room of family, friends, and nuns to laughter.

The plans hit a snag when we learned the church choir was unavailable. "We could always play the songs from a CD," Judy suggested, cheerful as ever. I pictured it and cringed.

Then my friend Lisa called from Washington. We'd met when our kids were in preschool and she'd ordered a huge batch of Mary Kay from me. We'd broken every sales rule that day—kids, wine, hours of chatting—and have been close ever since.

"Is there anything I can do?" she asked.

"Yes," I said. "Sing at Tom's Mass."

There was a pause. "I was thinking I could clean toilets or something," she said, laughing nervously. But she agreed.

On the day, Dylan gave the eulogy, sharing Tom's words from the last weeks of his life: "It's not about what you've accomplished but the moments you share with the people in your life." Hearing this made me smile inside; Tom had often felt he hadn't made a difference in the world. But Dylan's delivery—poised, heartfelt—proved otherwise.

Carlos, my brother-in-law, followed with his own heartfelt message. As he turned page after page, I smiled, imagining Tom's amused reaction.

Lisa sang *Amazing Grace* a cappella when the accompaniment went missing, then *On Eagle's Wings* with a couple of nuns joining in. The church was full—friends, neighbors, teammates, colleagues. I don't think Tom knew how many lives he'd touched.

After Mass, people came to our home. The kitchen buzzed

with conversation. In the backyard, two women from our meditation community offered sage healings; even the nuns took turns. Inside, the slideshow ran. Out front, Conor and Ryan played basketball with friends.

Then a colleague found me. "Tom's—or maybe your—brother is out front, bawling."

I stepped outside to see a dad from Conor's old team, sitting on the curb, crying.

"One day he's alive and joking with us, the next he's gone," he said. "I can take a funeral, hearing Dylan and Carlos speak—but that video… I can't believe he's gone."

"Me neither," I said. We cried together on the curb.

———

Lisa walks into the house carrying a large brown bag in her arms.

"It's time to get you good and drunk," she announces.

"What?"

"You told me you wanted to get drunk."

"I meant a bottle of red wine," I explain.

"That's too tame for today," she says. "In honor of your blue-eyed Irishman, I give you Irish Car Bombs: Guinness, Baileys Irish Cream, and Irish whiskey."

I'm not sure how well this grand plan is going to go. I can count the times I've been drunk on one hand. I can handle a bit more than a single beer or glass of wine, but I usually stop there. The line between Happy Julie, Bitchy Julie, and Puking Julie is blurry—it's just easier to be safe.

But the night after Tom's memorial, with my dear friend at my side, I'm easily swayed.

The irony isn't lost on me.

Earlier today, I'd put my head down and cried when the family raised their glasses. All day we had celebrated his life, but in that moment, it felt like celebrating his death—and something in me resisted it. I dropped my head into my hands and started bawling at the table.

Lisa pours Guinness into two large mugs, then fills two shot glasses with Baileys and whiskey.

"You have to drink it quickly so the cream doesn't curdle," she says, sliding the mug toward me and handing me the shot glass.

"How quickly?"

"Just don't sip it. This isn't wine."

My hand trembles as I hover the shot glass over the Guinness. I look up toward heaven.

"This is for you, Tom," I say, dropping the shot into the mug and drinking fast.

It's sweet and bitter all at once—like this moment, sitting with my friend, trying to drink away the bitterness of the day.

I don't stop at one Irish Car Bomb. I drink five.

Lisa and I are giggling up a storm when Dylan, Conor, and Ryan return from a movie. Dylan shakes his head.

"Oh no. She can't handle this," he says. "We need damage control."

Lisa nods and whips up the best grilled cheese sandwich I've ever had. Buttery, golden, and dripping onto the plate—I devour it along with two ibuprofen and a huge glass of water before heading to bed.

The following morning, I wake to our dog, Lucky's desperate bark. The house feels eerily empty. My head is clear —no worse than the fog I've lived in since watching Tom draw his last breath.

Lucky's not as fortunate. He spent the night gorging on leftovers from the hundred or so people who came to the house after the memorial. I let him out four times before grabbing the leash and taking him for a walk while everyone else sleeps.

The air is cool and still. As I walk, the night before drifts back in pieces. I think about the mug, about how I kept refilling it. Tom would have laughed.

The street is empty. I keep moving.

Chapter 13
The Wedding

Our wedding ceremony was very different from what I had dreamed it would be as a young girl. It was something short of a miracle that Tom had agreed to marry me after years of stressing that he did not want to marry again. He was very clear on this from the very beginning of our relationship.

"Don't fall in love with me, Julie. I am not the one," he'd said. "When you are ready to get married and have kids, there's the door."

It wasn't very romantic, but it was honest. The problem was that I'd already fallen in love with him.

Six years into our relationship, I sat on the edge of the bathtub, nervously waiting for the results to show on the home pregnancy test. My cycles had been a bit irregular for a while —probably from the stress of working twelve-hour night shifts in the Pediatric Intensive Care Unit (PICU) and obsessively taking dance classes of every kind—ballet, modern, jazz, and now Afro-Haitian—at the community college. I was still as uncoordinated as ever, but I loved it. My weight had dropped to 104 pounds—lighter than I'd been in high school.

I thought I might be pregnant because the motion sickness from sailing with friends the previous day persisted after I returned to land. During the few minutes waiting for the results, I prayed that the test would be negative.

I'd had two abortions at this point. The first, when I was seventeen, left me with nightmares. I often banged my head against the wall as a way to punish myself for it. After the second, I developed an infection so severe that the doctor warned I might not be able to have children. I couldn't go through that again. And I did, in fact, want to have kids some-day. The timing felt all wrong, yet I also wanted to hold onto Tom and the life we were building together. That push and pull kept me frozen as I waited for the test.

Minutes later, I stared at the two pink lines on the test stick and began to cry. Planned or not, pregnancy was a miracle, especially in my case. I began thinking about what changes I would need to make in order to make it work—most likely on my own.

When I told Tom, his reaction was immediate.

"How can you do this to us?" he demanded.

"There was never any guarantee with you," I shot back. "The baby is a sure thing."

The argument didn't resolve. We just stopped arguing.

Shortly afterward, Tom left on his motorcycle to meet up with his friend, Ed. Hours later, I got a phone call telling me he had slid out on some gravel on the shoulder of the freeway and was at the hospital. He was also under arrest for a DUI.

The weeks that followed were tense, and I still don't know what finally made him stay. Was it the motorcycle accident? The DUI? The fact that Tom couldn't work with a broken arm? Or did Ed convince him to stay?

Months later, I heard those words every girl dreams of hearing.

Just not how I imagined it.

"So…I guess we'll do this thing."

No big romantic moment. He stood in the doorway between the two rooms of our San Francisco flat and blurted it out like we were picking out a new paint color.

Tom quit smoking soon after finding out I was pregnant.

We began planning a small ceremony before the baby's birth. I imagined a night cruise on the San Francisco Bay—until a nightmare of Tom and me escaping on a dinghy, leaving behind my fighting parents and both families protesting our non-Catholic ceremony. That's when I came up with Plan B. The "B" standing for balloon.

I was receiving care at a free-standing birth center in Marin, and when our midwife heard about the balloon plan, she asked us to wait past twenty weeks—so that if a rough landing triggered labor, the baby would at least have a fighting chance.

———

Months later, the wedding day arrived. The hotel alarm went off far too early. Tom and Dylan went into the bathroom to get ready while I got dressed in the room. I should have been worried about the groom seeing me in my wedding dress before the ceremony. Instead, I slid a foot-long bungee cord into Tom's tuxedo pocket.

Much to my surprise, there was one already there.

It was rare that Tom and I thought alike, but today was different. Today, we were getting married—in a hot air balloon.

"I'm curious how you came up with the idea of getting married in a hot air balloon," our midwife had said.

"It took me so long to agree to marry her," Tom replied, "Julie wants to be sure the only way out is to bungee-jump off the side."

I smiled and slipped my own cord into the pocket—doubling the escape hatches.

That lightness would matter more than we knew.

Heavy fog in Yountville grounded the balloon. Wearing my wedding dress, I sat wringing my hands while the crew debated options. Instead of canceling, they drove us to farmland in Dixon along with a couple other balloon companies.

We watched crews take turns filling their balloons—blasts of fire swelling the fabric before the baskets tipped upright and lifted off.

Finally, it was our turn.

Dylan and I climbed into the basket to help keep it grounded while the men worked the ropes. I felt the baby kicking as we huddled together at the bottom of the basket.

Then a gust of wind caught the half-inflated balloon, dragging the basket across the field, men still clinging to the ropes while Dylan and I crouched inside. The pilot's foot was badly injured in the process.

The wind had picked up enough that it was no longer safe for our balloon to launch. The crew discussed options again, and I worried our wedding might not happen.

Our driver ushered the rest of us into the other van and we set off across the fields, chasing the company's second balloon, which had launched earlier that morning. He zigzagged Pac-Man-like through the rows of crops to meet it at the landing.

When it touched down, the passengers climbed out, the propane tanks were swapped, and we climbed in—Tom, Dylan, John and Mary, our ministers, me, and another woman who'd signed up for a ride that morning.

"Ready?" the pilot asked.

We nodded.

The ground fell away.

I smiled at my tall, dark-haired groom.

At cruising height, the ceremony began. Just before we were asked to say "I do," a drawn-out scream rang out.

We looked down to see a small group of people bungee-jumping off a crane. Tom pulled bungee cords from his pocket and grinned.

"I guess we won't be needing these," he said.

We laughed—and then we said "I do."

Chapter 14
Bitter Brew

The first sip of dark French roast hits my tongue with a familiar boldness—bitter, smoky, almost burnt at the edges. It has an earthy depth, like damp soil in early spring. Coffee used to be both invigorating and calming—a welcome jolt, the first step toward wakefulness and orientation. But now, after loss, it lands differently. The heat spreads across my tongue, but it doesn't spark my body to life. It lingers, dull and distant. The ritual is still there, but the comfort is muted.

Tom and I liked our coffee strong and black. In the early years of our relationship, Tom was pursuing a master's degree in English literature at San Jose State University (SJSU), and I was trying to get into the nursing program at De Anza College. We spent hours in coffee shops, sipping double cappuccinos and studying together. In high school, I'd been a C student, never confident in my smarts. The nursing program felt out of reach—too competitive for someone like me. But Tom believed in me when I couldn't. His faith quieted the doubt. I did the work, but his belief made it possible. I graduated at the top of my class.

In our dating years, Tom often took the lead—choosing

where we'd go, what we'd eat, how to fill the little spaces between studying and work. We spent hours in coffee shops or on the beach with books spread between us, and I was always happy to do "whatever you want." As a middle child, I'd become an expert at going with the flow—so good at it, back then, I sometimes forgot to have opinions of my own.

One night, while we were deciding on pizza toppings, Tom looked at me and said he wished I'd want things for myself more often. "It's okay to disagree," he told me. "It's natural."

Years later, after we were married and the boys were still young, that lesson came back to him. I don't even remember what we were arguing about—something small, I'm sure—but I wasn't backing down. We were upstairs in our little Cupertino home, voices rising and echoing off the walls. I stood with my hands on my hips, chest puffed out like a boxer before the bell, standing on my tiptoes to look taller than I was.

"Remember," I yelled, "you told me I didn't always have to agree with you—and I don't!"

A slow smile spread across his face, and then he laughed. Just like that, the fight was over. We must have found a compromise; I only remember that laughter and the relief that followed. For once, I'd stood my ground—and he loved me for it.

Fifteen years later, after being overbid on house after house, we finally were able to purchase our first home. By this time Dylan was already away at college, and as first-time buyers we needed more space than a typical starter home could offer. Interest rates were high, inventory was low, and we paid top price for this four-bedroom house where I now sit, drinking my morning coffee—alone.

I'm on the couch instead of in bed, where I used to sip while Tom shaved and showered for work. We took turns making the French roast, pour-over method, producing two strong, black cups of bold, rich goodness. I miss his smiling blue eyes lighting up as he set the warm cup on the bedside table, the peck on the cheek, and the "good morning" before he took over the bathroom.

As I head upstairs with my second cup of coffee, I hear Conor in the bathroom. The fog in my head swirls. I've waited for clarity and energy to arrive, but all I'm left with is the aftertaste—acrid, dry, almost metallic.

It started as another small, stupid thing I said—some comment that slipped out sideways, half-jealous, half-tired. I'd made a crack about one of the women Tom worked with, and he called me on it.

"I'm not going to fix it by telling you you're beautiful," he said. "If you can't see it, how can I? Go look in the mirror, Julie. Really look."

Then he walked out, leaving me stewing on the bed. I sat there for a few minutes, arms crossed, sulking like a child. The house was quiet except for the faint sound of the boys down the hall. Finally, I stood and went into the tiny bathroom.

The words stung. I'd wanted comfort, not truth. But I was asking Tom to fix something that wasn't his to fix.

When I looked, really looked, I saw what I always saw first —the dark circles, the tired eyes, the soft belly that never quite went away after pregnancy. I almost turned off the light. Then I lingered. My hair was thick and dark, my brows full, my lashes long. The light hit my face and, beneath those dark circles, my green eyes sparked something deep inside. I saw that I was still beautiful.

A soft smile spread across my face. There she was—the woman Tom fell in love with. She'd been there all along; I just hadn't seen her.

When he came to bed, I was already half-asleep. He rolled toward me and wrapped his arm around me.

Chapter 15
Holding It Together

I wake to the sound of Conor getting ready for school, and a rush of sadness hits me. I wipe away the tears as I open the door to his room.

"You don't have to go to school today if you don't want to," I tell him.

"I know," he says, "I need to be with my friends."

I nod, wipe away another tear, and close the door, trying not to feel the sting of not being the one he turns to. Even before high school, Conor had been more connected to his friends than us. Ryan is the opposite. He only wants to be with me and does not want to go to school for the first few days. He is quiet and wants to sleep a lot. I go back to my room to wake him up.

Even before Tom died, Ryan would often have terrible nightmares, screaming in the hallway and shaking in a panic. After Tom died, his nightmares got worse. He became afraid to go to sleep, waking in tears from dreams of death—Tom's, mine, Conor's, and his own. Since then, he's slept beside me most nights.

Before Tom got sick, Ryan made a game out of claiming his dad's "spot" in our bed on the weekends. He—and sometimes Conor—would climb in beside me for story time. After the story ended, Ryan would pretend to be asleep and wait for Tom to come.

"WHO is sleeping in MY SPOT?" Tom would roar, Billy Goat Gruff style.

With his head buried under the covers, a quiet giggle could be heard.

"Who…is sleeping in my spot?"

Another giggle.

Then came the tickles of the covers, until Ryan couldn't take it any longer. Afterwards, Ryan and Tom went down the hall where Tom would tuck him in, then open the door to Conor's room to say, "Good night."

I bend down and gently wake Ryan. "You can stay in your PJs but I have to take Conor to school and you need to come with me," I say.

Conor doesn't usually wake up easily—or on his own. I suspect he didn't sleep well. We pile into the minivan and drive to school. Conor says he will grab breakfast at school, so we are uncharacteristically early for drop off. I watch him cross the street, approach the school campus, and meet up with one of his friends. His friend gives him a hug.

Later in the day, Ryan talks about his dad in heaven.

"Grandma and Grandpa Fergus will be happy to see him again," he tells me. "Dad will be happy to see his friend David and that guy who had the horses."

I listen, as he shares possible scenarios of life in heaven.

"He'll visit with them a while and then come back to earth to join a new family, in a new body, when he is ready," he says.

I'm struck by the way he blends it all together.

This thought seems to comfort him—for a while—but later, he's sad again.

"What if Dad, in his new body, doesn't know me?"

I hug my son, grateful that I can offer him a little comfort in the moment.

Conor keeps most of what he's feeling to himself, or to his friends. His baseball teammates and coaches offer their support—many of them having met Tom—and even his friends from our old neighborhood message to offer their support. But only a few of them could relate to such deep loss.

Unlike the schools where we used to live, Conor's new school carried different realities. Dress code restrictions prohibiting red and blue made it clear there were gang concerns here—something I hadn't encountered in our previous schools. Some of his schoolmates had already lost parents or siblings to violence. One had been shot for being in the wrong place at the wrong time.

Because I want Conor to feel free to come to me for comfort and support, I try to hold my emotions at bay in front of him. I'm not okay, but I push down the sadness, the sense that I'm carrying this alone, and fear of not being enough until I am alone. I am afraid of burdening my grieving sons with too much of my own pain. They have enough to carry and I don't want them to feel like they have to take care of me —especially Conor.

I don't want the boys to worry about money either— although I am definitely worried. Before the cancer took away his ability to speak, Tom tried to reassure me that I would be okay if I cut back on unnecessary expenses like gym member- ships, eating take-out, and gourmet coffees.

"Take the life insurance and pay off the second," he told me. "You can just make the interest-only payment on the main loan. Wait for the interest rates to drop, then refinance."

Now I'm trying to make sense of it all—what I'm eligible for, what I can afford to lose. Three days of paid bereavement. After that, no pay. If I'm out more than thirty days, I'll have to cover our insurance premiums myself to avoid losing coverage.

———

The week after Tom's death, Ryan goes back to school.

By mid-morning, the school nurse calls and suggests it might be best if I come get him.

When I walk into the front office, the woman at the desk looks up. Her expression shifts when she sees me. She lowers her voice.

"I'm so sorry," she says.

The nurse steps out from behind the counter and touches my arm briefly. Another staff member glances over, then back down at her computer.

"He's not disruptive," she says gently. "He's just… sitting there. Blank. He's not engaging. We didn't know what else to do."

Blank.

I nod. It makes sense. I'm now doing the same thing most days—moving through tasks with a face that doesn't feel like mine.

They ask me to wait.

I sit in one of the molded plastic chairs against the wall. The office hums with phones ringing and printers spitting out paper. A child walks in late with a parent. Another is sent back to class with an ice pack pressed to his forehead.

I stare at nothing.

After a few minutes, the office door opens and Ryan walks toward me.

He doesn't cry. He doesn't look up. He just comes and stands beside my chair.

We don't say much. We don't have to.

We walk out together.

Just outside the minivan, as I open the sliding door, he turns suddenly and folds into me.

The sobs come fast and hard, his small body shaking against mine. I hold him there in the parking lot, one hand cradling the back of his head, the other pressed between his shoulder blades. The world keeps moving around us—cars pulling in and out, children laughing somewhere beyond the fence.

I don't try to fix it. I don't tell him it will be okay. I just hold him.

The next day, he makes it through school.

By Wednesday afternoon, he's back on the baseball field.

I watch as Ryan climbs out of the minivan, grabs his bat bag, and jogs toward the baseball field. His cleats clack against the pavement, the sound fading as he disappears toward the dugout. The late afternoon sun slants low, baking the infield and casting long shadows over the grass. The air smells faintly of cut grass and dust, the kind that coats your tongue when the wind picks up.

Several baseball moms settle into the metal bleachers, water bottles in hand, their voices lifting in the easy chatter. Others drive off to run errands before practice ends. I decide to run. I pull my hair into a ponytail, the elastic snapping against my wrist, and take several gulps from my water bottle. My shoes feel heavy, but the thought of sitting in the stands feels heavier.

Running steadies me for an hour. Then it's back to logistics and loss.

Over the first week, I do my best to navigate all the necessary "paperwork" like social security and DMV. I started cancelling memberships—or trying to. My gym membership was easy to cancel. Tom's was not.

"You just log into his account and complete the cancelation online," they tell me.

I take a deep breath, pausing in an effort not to yell at the kid on the phone.

"My husband died and I do not have his password."

"Umm. Maybe he wrote it down somewhere," he says.

I am irritated and exhausted from recounting how quickly Tom went from healthy to unable to speak.

"Yeah, right!"

I hung up, wishing that it had been more dramatic, like slamming the headset on the receiver instead of pressing the end call button.

I can't seem to get anything done. My brain feels thick, like it's wrapped in fog, and I'm always forgetting something—keys, appointments, whole conversations. The thought of going back to work full time makes my chest tighten. I don't know how I'm going to hold it all together.

Then, out of nowhere, kindness shows up. Conor's baseball Team Mom started a meal train. She even tracked down families from our old neighborhood to help. Starting Monday, dinners will land on our doorstep three nights a week.

When she asked what kinds of meals we liked, I froze. I knew we had favorites. We must have. But I couldn't pull them up. Pasta? Chicken? Tacos? Even those felt like decisions too large to make. I heard myself say, "Anything is fine." And I meant it. The relief wasn't about the food. It was about not having to choose.

It doesn't make the grief easier, but it lifts one small weight.

Finding Stride
Navigating Early Grief

Chapter 16
Weighted Miles

The minivan door slams shut, the sound echoing across the parking lot. I stand there for a moment, keys heavy in my palm, wondering if I have the energy left to run. I clip them to the inside hook of my vest, zip the pocket, and tug the handle to make sure it's locked.

It's been just over a week since Tom died, and already I'm forgetting the things I used to do without thinking—locking doors, setting oven timers.

Monday, I tell myself I've had a productive day, but everywhere I look, half-finished jobs stare back: Ryan's bed stripped but unmade, an empty toilet paper holder lying beside the roll, laundry sitting in the open washer in the garage. Each job abandoned for the next—pulled to the bathroom by a full bladder, to the cupboard by an empty roll, to the phone by a ringing landline.

This isn't productive. This is surviving—barely.

Tuesday, I'm in the dentist's chair for my cleaning. I close my eyes and there he is—Tom's blue eyes looking right into mine. My breath catches.

"Am I hurting you?" the hygienist asks, removing the cleaning tool.

I shake my head.

When I close my eyes again, he's gone.

The rest of the staff file in, one by one, with hugs and condolences.

"He's in a better place," one says.

I look away before my frustration spills over. *What could be better than being with his wife and kids?* I force a half smile.

My dentist finally appears.

"We were shocked," he says. "He was so young."

I nod, unable to speak. Sunglasses on, I leave as fast as I can.

The weekend can't come fast enough, even knowing Monday—my first day back at work—will arrive too soon. Maybe if I can run, I can believe I'll get through a full day at work.

I start by walking. The chill in the air nips at my cheeks, whispering the same questions I've been asking myself: Am I tough enough to go on without him? Can I raise two boys alone? I tighten my ponytail, take a breath, and push into a slow run. I don't have a choice, I tell myself. I am all they have.

My feet slap the pavement, heavy and graceless—the kind of sound that usually gets under my skin. My legs feel like they belong to someone else. I'm weighted down with sadness, with too little sleep, with the weight of keeping the boys well fed, helping with homework, and trying to offer them hope when I can't seem to find my own.

I try to focus on myself: the sound of my own footfall, my breath, my body and mind. But my mind is a blurred mess of thoughts.

Up ahead, a dad pushes a stroller toward the playground, a mom jogging beside a child on a bike. The sight tugs me backward—to Tom and me training for our first marathon.

I can smell sunscreen, feel the sway of the stroller handle under my palms. We had a system: Tom took off first while I packed snacks, diapers for Ryan, and gels for Tom and me. I kept my hydration pack looped over the stroller handle, the tube dangling near Ryan's mouth. More than once he'd suck it dry without me noticing. I'd only realize when his diaper felt twice its size.

Ryan rode in the stroller, Conor pedaling beside us on his little bike. We'd catch Tom, the boys high-fiving him as we passed.

At each playground we'd pause for a play break—hanging out until Tom caught up. I'd watch the boys play until it was time to run again—after Tom passed through, grabbing a gel from the stroller pocket before heading out again. Sometimes it was messy, but it worked.

On race day in Napa, we each ran our own race, different paces, same finish line.

A gust of wind snaps me back.

I pass the playground where the boys and I once waited for Tom, and the familiarity stings. Same path. But everything else has changed.

My legs ache like I'm starting from zero—because in a way, I am. I focus on my breath, the cold air scraping at my throat, the steady rhythm of inhale and exhale. Gradually, something inside me settles.

My arms feel loose now, my stride a little easier. Even weighted down, my body remembers what to do.

For a few strides, I swear I feel him running next to me. He could never keep up before, but now he's free from the limits of his body. My pace slows, and I hear him in my mind —*I love you, Julie*—in flashes from our years together. Tears mix with sweat, stinging my eyes.

I walk, then run again. The cool air bites at my lungs. I keep moving. Whether I'm walking or running, forward is still forward.

Chapter 17
Playing the Long Game

When I was little, dinner in our house meant the TV was on and conversation was discouraged. One night, eager to share a success story from school, I started talking before my mom's show came back from commercial.

"Julie," she said, annoyed, "we didn't turn on the TV to listen to you."

I poked at my food and went quiet.

As the third of four kids, I'd figured out how family math worked. Someone always had to give way. I learned early that if I didn't want much, I'd never be disappointed. Pizza toppings? I liked everything. "You can choose," I'd say.

That habit stuck. Even now, I conserve energy—holding back words, sidestepping arguments that might not be worth the effort.

Because of Tom's long workdays, much of the child-rearing fell to me. I had a full-time job managing clinical trials at a pharmaceutical company, which meant regular travel. Still, being present for my boys mattered more to me than keeping score.

On one trip, I called home to check in with Tom and tell the boys I missed them.

"Dad made the best chicken tacos ever!" Ryan announced, his voice bubbling with excitement.

"Really?" I asked.

"Yeah. You can go on another work trip if you want. Dad can make us chicken tacos again."

I could hear Tom laughing in the background. He was still laughing when he got on the phone. He didn't brag. He didn't have to. I knew the praise thrilled him.

My parents missed most of my sporting events and rarely made time for the big milestones. Because of that, I made a point of being present at my kids' events whenever possible.

On his days off, Tom preferred long bike rides, working on his latest writing, or strumming his guitar, while I ran back and forth between the boys' baseball fields. I squeezed my marathon training into those practice windows so I didn't have to ask him to stay home with the boys while I ran—not that he wouldn't have.

His work didn't end when he walked through the door. Some nights he stayed up until midnight to catch his team in India at the start of their day, hoping they would prioritize his requests.

I learned to measure what he had left before asking for more.

Tom understood the demands of marathon training. We had trained for and completed our first few marathons together, before his body started to protest. But running was hard on Tom's 6'2", 200-plus-pound frame; his shins, hips, and spine didn't tolerate the pounding. He decided to lose some weight before trying again. These were the same areas where tumors would later show up on scans.

On game days, Tom usually chose Conor's baseball game —it was more competitive—while Ryan's was still at the fun-to-fun stage, the younger league where the score didn't matter.

If there were volunteer shifts, those fell to me. Other families seemed to have more fatherly involvement, but this wasn't a battle I wanted to fight.

Tom was always there when it mattered—for me, for the kids, or anyone who needed him. Once, after I told him about a family I visited as a home nurse—a home with nothing more than a few mattresses on the floor and a beat up crib—he loaded our gently used futon into the truck, along with new sheets and blankets. We delivered them together. The family was so grateful, they insisted on feeding us homemade soup before we left.

Parenting, marriage, work—it's all a constant recalibration. Choosing when to push and when to let go. Distance running teaches you the same thing—how to conserve your energy, how to save enough for the long haul. That balance feels even more fragile now, with Tom gone and the boys looking to me for everything. Monday will test a different kind of endurance.

Chapter 18
Finding My Way Back

I have been dreading my first day back at work. It isn't the work itself; it's facing the people.

Emotionally, I feel like a blister rubbed raw from too many miles. I think about how the boys returned to school almost immediately after Tom died, and now I wonder if they had it right. At least then, it made sense to cry at any moment.

The traffic is light; the neighboring school district is on spring break. I arrive thirty minutes earlier than expected, pull into a parking spot, and turn off the car. My heart pounds, and I sit frozen, watching my coworker head inside. I wait until she's gone before following.

Inside, my desk is exactly as I left it—neat, orderly, a small stack of non-confidential papers, and two framed photos of Tom and the kids. But in the center sits something new: a bright yellow miniature rose plant.

It's meant as kindness, but it hits me sideways.

In the days after Tom died, my house overflowed with flowers—lilies, roses, tall vases of tropical blooms—many sent by people I barely knew. Their beauty pierced me. They lived on, even as he didn't.

The rose bush on my desk is alive too, but different.

Because it's potted, it carries a quiet promise of endurance. Maybe it won't wilt in a week. Maybe it doesn't have to die. But it's also a reminder: things aren't the same. I didn't just take a vacation and return unchanged.

The first tear falls.

The rest of the day offers no mercy. I'm locked out of the network. My mouse doesn't work. Emails have piled up like unopened mail from another life. The hours pass faster than expected, though I accomplish almost nothing. I tell myself that's okay. I'm laying the groundwork. I feel untethered but functional—until two o'clock.

I'm stepping out of the bathroom just as someone I barely know steps in. She stops, surprised.

"Oh, hi Julie. I didn't know you were back. I'm so sorry about your husband."

"Thank you," I manage.

She goes on—her father had lung cancer too. It spread to his brain—six years later. She says she knows exactly what I'm going through.

But she doesn't. She can't. Her story hangs between us, well-meaning but intrusive. I nod, make a vague sound, and find my exit.

After that, I ask my boss if I can leave. I grab my running clothes from my bag, change, and drive to the open space preserve where Tom and I spent many weekends doing our long runs.

The gravel crunches under my tires. I slam the van door harder than necessary, tie my shoes tighter than usual, and head out.

A mile in, I reach the steep hill and attack it like I'm mad at the world—which I am.

At cancer and the silence he left behind.

The hill rises for two miles, demanding everything I've got. My calves burn. My pulse and breath quicken. The sun beats down on my shoulders, the wind offers no relief. I don't care that it hurts. The hurt reminds me I'm still here.

Up, up, up I go. Each step is effort, each breath thick with memory. I run and sob at the same time. I think of Tom. Of all I've lost. Of everything I still carry. I tell myself I'd climb as high as heaven for one more kiss, one more hug. The ache rises so high it almost feels like wanting to follow him.

But I also know—I'm not ready to leave. Not yet. I still have work to do—two boys who need me here.

My pace slows, but I don't stop. The sky stretches clear and blue above me, cloudless and indifferent. When I reach the top, the view steals my breath—not just from the climb, but from the beauty. Hills roll in every direction, golden and green. The world, even through heartache, still holds wonder. And I am still part of it.

By week's end, I've shown up. I've answered some emails, read through my project documents. But it doesn't feel like work yet. I'm still half-submerged.

In the mornings, I find myself reaching for the same things over and over—black pants, a gray shirt, maybe white. The brighter colors hang off to one side of the closet, untouched. I don't make a decision about it; my hand just goes where it goes. It's easier that way. Later, I'll realize how long it takes before I reach for anything else.

During a three-hour training session, the department director asks if I'll join a task force for an upcoming project. I say yes before I even know what it's about. My head is fogged in grief, and the slides don't make it any easier. Acronyms fill every page—CRDM, EDS, SGL-7, QIDS—like a foreign language.

It isn't just the acronyms. Something else is off.

A colleague introduces herself before the meeting. I hear her name. I nod. We begin talking. And before she's finished her second sentence, I realize I've already lost it. The name is gone. Not misplaced—gone. I keep listening, smiling, pretending I'll remember it in a moment. I don't.

This starts happening everywhere. Someone gives me instructions and halfway through, the first part slips away. I open an email, read it twice, and still can't hold the details long enough to respond.

If I don't write something down immediately, it evaporates. I start carrying a notebook everywhere. When I can't jot something down, I try to tether it to something familiar—a rhyme, a face, a childhood image. If someone says their name is Ernie, I picture Bert and Ernie standing side by side on Sesame Street, hoping the image will glue the name in place. Sometimes it works. Often it doesn't.

It's embarrassing. And frightening. I was never like this before.

Tom would have made a joke. He always reached for humor when things felt unbearable. Even in the hospital, when nothing made sense, he found a way to laugh.

Maybe that's what I'm doing—stirring the soup with a little sarcasm, trying to taste some resilience. If I can laugh, even a little, maybe I won't break.

This weekend, I lace up again and head out. The air is cool—the kind that wakes you before the coffee does. My footfall is quiet and easy against the pavement, the stillness broken only by the hum of distant traffic, a dog barking somewhere up ahead, and the occasional walker or runner passing by.

Today's run is short; the boys' games matter more, and I want to be there for every inning. Tomorrow, I'll go longer. I'll climb that hill at the preserve, let the air fill my lungs, let the ache settle into my legs. But for now, it's just me and the road —steady, uncomplicated, and mine.

Chapter 19
The Act of Showing Up

The door to the minivan slides into place after I try—and fail—to slam it shut. The effect lacks the drama I crave—no satisfying thud, just the soft glide of a mechanism built for efficiency. It's quiet. Too quiet.

I've been back at work for two weeks now. A new rhythm is taking shape. The boys are back into their school and sports routine, and I'm back to ticking items off my never-ending to-do list.

With his shirt half tucked, half hanging loose, Ryan warms up in the fading light with his teammates. He's started to join in again, and even laugh once in a while, and I wonder if he takes after me—hiding sadness behind a smile.

The air smells like fresh-cut grass. I suppress a sneeze and take a deep breath. Three miles before dinner. My heart pounds—not from effort, not yet—but from everything else stacked on the day.

I took today off work to handle things. To get through the kind of tasks that pile up when someone dies. First, the gym. I finally canceled Tom's membership. Unlike the first time I called—when the guy told me to just figure out Tom's password—this time I wasn't asking. I walked into the gym with the death certificate in hand and refused to leave until it was done.

Then, the Social Security office. I showed up with my documents, ready to sit across from someone and handle the benefits paperwork for the boys. I'd made the appointment online a few days earlier. What I'd forgotten—or misunderstood—was that it was a phone appointment. Scheduled for tomorrow.

Instead of crossing something off my list, I wasted half the morning standing in the wrong line, holding the right papers for the wrong day.

Now I run.

Not for a race. Not for Boston. Not yet.

The streets that loop around the ball field are familiar, but today they feel heavier beneath my feet, like they know. Each step carries weight—grief, exhaustion, the running list of everything that's now mine to carry.

Tom used to help Conor with math homework. He was so good at it—calm, focused, patient. I try, but I don't have his gift for numbers. Especially now, when even small problems feel bigger than they should.

Halfway through the second loop, my throat tightens. I swallow hard and keep going.

I turn the corner and the field comes back into view.

Ryan is still running drills with his team. I slow to a walk, breath catching, legs tight and sore.

———

After Ryan was born, I returned from maternity leave to find my discharge coordinator role gone. I was back to home visits —many of them to adult cystic fibrosis patients. Each appointment required rigorous chest percussion—twelve positions, repeated again and again. My wrists absorbed every strike. The patients were scattered across the Bay Area. Hours of driving. Hours of pounding.

Before long, my wrists began to give out. I couldn't even hold my baby without pain. That's when I knew something had to change.

I applied for a pediatric research nurse position and was hired onto an ADHD trial. It was new and energizing. When the trial ended, I decided to move into industry—to the monitoring side of research.

After the interviews, the offer came. The manager's voice was bright and efficient. The number was lower than I'd expected. Heat rose in my face. I thought about asking for more. The words stalled somewhere between my chest and my throat.

Don't be ungrateful, the voice in my head said. *You should be glad they want you at all.*

So I thanked her. I accepted.

When I got home, I told Tom what had happened. He didn't make a big deal of it—just shook his head and said I had to believe I was worth more. I wanted to, but I didn't yet know how.

Later, I learned I was the lowest paid in my role. I didn't protest. I worked harder instead.

I took pride in working independently—never complaining, never reminding anyone of the extra hours. That habit followed me as my career evolved. I was dependable, steady, invisible in the way dependable people often are.

Years later, I sat in the front row of a company-wide meeting celebrating a stretch goal. Completing two key Phase I clinical trials before year's end had taken everything I had.

When the slide appeared, my name wasn't there.

The sting was familiar enough that it didn't surprise me.

I'd long since learned that silence has its price. Recognition isn't always the reward for doing good work. At some point, quiet competence had turned into disappearing.

Chapter 20
Benign

My throat tightens as I hold the envelope in my hand. I already know it isn't good news.

In the hallway, someone is crying. Someone else murmurs, *I'm so sorry.* The air feels thin, charged, like before a storm.

I tell myself not to panic. Don't spiral. Not here. Not now.

I open it slowly. The paper trembles. The first paragraph blurs—*restructuring, alignment, transition period.*

I scan for a date.

There isn't one.

Three months since Tom died. And now this.

HR offers résumé workshops and interview coaching, as if bullet points can steady a life already knocked sideways. I sit under fluorescent lights, rewriting myself into phrases like "results-driven" and "strategic thinker," while my insides feel hollow.

Then comes word of another merger. One building. More reshuffling. More uncertainty. The ground keeps shifting.

———

Then I find the lump.

I'm in the shower when my fingers catch on something that wasn't there before. Steam fogs the mirror. Water runs over my shoulders. I press again, slower this time.

There.

Small. Hard. Deep.

I shift my arm, change angles, press from above. Maybe it's nothing. Maybe I'm imagining it.

I am not imagining it.

I am standing naked under hot water, bargaining with my own body.

My boys need me.

Not this too.

I message my doctor. Within hours, appointments are scheduled—mammogram, ultrasound. I watch the technicians' faces for clues. The radiologist says little. "Follow up with a surgeon."

That's enough.

The next day, I see the surgeon. After reviewing the images, he schedules surgery for the following week.

There's no room for delay. I'm the only parent my boys have left. Since Tom's death, I drive far more cautiously, check and recheck crosswalks, treat every headache like it could turn catastrophic. Conor and Ryan need me. I cannot take chances.

On the day of my surgery, my mom drives me to the hospital. That in itself feels strange. I'm not used to her showing up this way. But today, she shows up. Drives. Waits. Sits quietly in the waiting room while I'm prepped for surgery.

Inside the operating room, the lights blaze white and clinical. Nurses move around trays of gleaming instruments, faces hidden behind masks, gowns rustling as they work. Someone adjusts something near my IV. Someone else reassures me I'm in good hands. Music plays softly in the background—something light and familiar, though I can't place it. I'm not sure if

I'm completely out, but I remember my heart pounding, my breath deliberate under those bright, humming lights.

I'm not afraid of the procedure. I'm afraid of what they'll find. Of the word I don't say aloud—cancer. I am afraid of what it would mean for my boys if I don't survive it. They've already lost their father. They will not lose me too.

A nurse touches my arm and smiles beneath her mask. "You're doing great," she says.

I nod. Grateful for her kindness. Grateful for my stubborn, protective will to survive.

In recovery, I feel groggy, slightly outside my body, as though floating just above it. I'm relieved it's over. I vomit once before they clear me to go home, where my mom drives me back in the same quiet way she brought me. I hold it together—mostly. A few tears slide down my cheeks in the car, but I don't fully break until we pull into my driveway.

When her car backs out of the driveway—engine rumbling, tires bumping over the curb—I crack open. The sobs come from somewhere deep, from every pocket of fear I've held down. *What if I do have cancer? What happens to my boys? How will their lives be without me?*

I let myself fall apart just long enough to feel it, then force myself to pull it back together. I have to pick the boys up from school. I have to be fine—for them.

The biopsy results come about a week later. I've been on edge, flinching every time the phone rings. When the doctor finally calls, I brace myself, heart hammering.

"Benign," he says.

"Benign?" I repeat, needing to hear it twice.

"Yes. You're fine," he reassures. "Keep doing your monthly exams."

I hang up and exhale a breath I feel like I've been holding for days. It's not over—not the grief, not the layoffs, not the uncertainty—but at least this isn't the start of another loss. I'm still here. For now, that is everything.

That evening, I take the boys out to dinner.

It feels like a splurge, something I haven't allowed much since Tom died. I've been watching every dollar, quietly calculating how long I can stretch things. But tonight calls for something else. I need to mark the moment with the simple joy of being with my boys, safe and intact.

We slide into a booth at our favorite Mexican restaurant— the same place Tom and I took them for last days of school. The booth's vinyl sticks to the backs of our legs. Chips and salsa sit between us. The air smells of grilled meat and warm tortillas. I wait until their food is in front of them, then tell them.

"A few weeks ago, I found a breast lump and had it checked out," I say.

Conor holds his breath; Ryan's face goes pale.

"They took it out and tested it and it's not cancer," I tell them.

"So… you're going to be okay?" Ryan asks.

"Yes," I say. "I'm fine."

They both climb out of the booth and wrap their arms around me.

Chapter 21
What's Missing

I sit at the kitchen table filling out another form.

Name. Address. Emergency contact.

Marital status.

My pen hovers over the boxes. Married. Single. Divorced. None of them fit.

I look down at my left hand. The gold band presses into my skin, warm from my body. I twist it, back and forth.

Tom is gone. But I am not single.

I draw my own square and write widowed beside it.

The word looks thin on the page. Insufficient.

Still, drawing the box feels like a small protest. As if I'm correcting the form. As if I'm educating whoever designed it. There should be a place for us.

A plate of food sits beside me, untouched. I take a bite because I know I should. It tastes like cardboard. I chew and swallow without appetite.

Across the table, Tom's chair sits pushed in neatly, as if he's stepped away for a moment. I catch myself staring at it longer than I mean to.

I push the papers aside.

Upstairs, I change into running clothes. My jeans slide off

more easily than they used to. Not dramatic. Not skeletal. Just looser. Grief has taken its portion.

I lace my shoes.

I run because I need to.

Because movement is the only thing that steadies me.

Because if I sit too long, the silence gets loud.

I run in small windows of time—during Ryan's baseball practices, between pickup and dinner—trying to burn off the ache that settles in my chest.

It doesn't burn off.

———

It's Open House at the elementary school. I walk from home, following the line of neighborhood parents. I'm grateful that our running late means we don't have time to catch up on each other's lives. I smile and wave as we file into the various classrooms.

As usual, the walls and ceilings are decorated with colorful displays of what students have been learning—or trying to learn. I wander from wall to wall, scanning the colorful projects and essays for Ryan's name—but I can't find any.

At his desk, everything is lined up neatly, probably for the parents' benefit. His books are stacked from largest to smallest; a few sharpened pencils, a small eraser, and a couple of his Yu-Gi-Oh cards—like the ones he got for Christmas—are all arranged neatly. I notice that there are folders of work on top of all the other desks. Ryan's has none.

The teacher sits behind her desk, cheerfully meeting with each of the parents. The line is long, but I wait, running my hand over the smooth desktop in an attempt to soothe my nerves.

When she sees me, she smiles softly and reaches into her desk for the folder.

"I have Ryan's work here," she says, motioning me over to her desk.

Some are almost finished, others trail off mid-paragraph or stop after a single line.

"He's doing his best," she adds, her voice kind. "It's just been hard for him to stay focused this year."

She pauses, choosing her words carefully. "We've decided it's best to move him on to third grade. He's bright—we don't want to hold him back and make things harder."

I nod, grateful for her tenderness, though part of me sinks. I know the feeling—starting projects, then leaving them half done.

As I walk out, the hallway is quieter now, the air still warm from the crowd that's passed through. I stop at the door and glance back at the rows of small desks. His desk sits waiting, perfectly arranged, as if neatness could disguise what's missing.

Chapter 22
Not Enough

Grief didn't just hollow me out. It also made me reach.

Over the past five years, I'd run eight marathons. Tom joined me for the first three, but the pounding took a toll on his body. He went back to cycling, hoping to drop some weight. I kept running. Kept chasing my dream of qualifying for the Boston Marathon.

I missed it again and again.

Some races unraveled early—you know by mile ten that the day is lost. Other times, the goal stays just within reach. If I pushed harder, hurt more, maybe I could still get there. And sometimes, even when I did, the clock said I'd still fallen short.

I've felt this before.

Back when I was in fifth grade—the smell of fresh-cut grass on the school field. I'm in a dress because my mom insists—one of the handmade ones my grandmother sewed— never quite right for climbing trees or racing boys. Lined up beside Eric—the fastest kid at our school—for yet another sprint. Day after day, we've battled it out. That last day, I push harder, lungs burning, and finally beat him. One win is enough.

The next afternoon I'm on the monkey bars with my girl-friends when Eric shows up, hands on his hips.

"Aren't we going to race today?"

I shrug. I don't need to. I've already won.

I've been chasing that feeling ever since—the certainty that I can push past the edge and take something that once felt out of reach. But Boston isn't fifth grade. One win isn't enough. The time has to meet a standard—on a certified course, under official clocks.

Boston is one of the highest honors in distance running—you can't just sign up for; you have to earn your way in. When I first started chasing a Boston Qualifier (BQ) in 2002, the standard for women ages thirty-five to thirty-nine was 3:45. That number didn't budge during the years I chased it. The only thing that changed was me. By 2007, I had aged into the next bracket. At forty-one, the qualifying time eased to 3:50.

That time became more than a number. It was discipline. Hope. Something solid to reach for when everything else felt unsteady. Boston wasn't just a race. It was an invitation to keep going. And even with the clock adjusted for my age, I still had a long way to go—maybe farther than I wanted to admit.

After Tom dies, the numbers don't disappear. If anything, they steady me. A standard doesn't bend for grief. Either you meet it, or you don't. There's something clean about that.

Chicago is already on my calendar. Tom and I picked it together last fall, imagining a family trip: visiting his relatives, cousins at the finish, deep-dish pizza and lakefront walks.

I could withdraw. No one would question it.

But pulling out would feel like erasing something we planned. One more thing undone.

So I don't.

I will run it.

Chapter 23
Father's Day
Without Fathers

The grocery store aisle is lined with Father's Day cards —Best Dad Ever, World's Greatest. I steer the cart past them without slowing down.

Father's Day hits hard this year—too hard. It's not just Tom. My stepfather died young too. The losses press against each other—two absences that shouldn't exist.

I plan a movie for the afternoon—something light, something contained. I run first, before the day can catch me.

Ryan is already off with a friend's family for the morning. Conor mumbles from his room when I tell him I'll be back before lunch. They don't mention what day it is. Neither do I.

The weather is perfect—sunny but still cool. One of those crisp June mornings that almost lets me believe everything is fine. I grab my gear and drive to meet Cindy, a coworker-turned-running partner, and her friend Fred in a nearby town with cafés and tree-lined streets.

So far, so good—until I switch on the radio. Father's Day tributes. Montages of kids thanking their dads. The gratitude stings. I turn it off.

I can't run away from this day.

When I arrive, the sidewalks are full. Families drift past in their Sunday clothes, unhurried. Fathers lift toddlers onto their shoulders.

We run nine miles together. When Cindy and Fred peel off, I keep going. Five more alone. The hills tug at my knees. I adjust. I always adjust.

Later that afternoon, I take the boys to see *Surf's Up*. I chose it because it looks light—animated penguins, bright colors, something contained. It starts slow but turns sweet. At one point, a character talks about losing someone important. I stiffen. I glance at the boys without letting them see me look. Blue light flickers across their faces. They don't move. They keep watching. So do I.

Back home, I start packing for a week long camp the boys will be going to next week. In Ryan's room, I spread the packing list on the carpet and build two piles—one for Conor, one for Ryan. Conor drifts in and out with items from his room. Ryan stays, choosing things with me. The dog lies between the two piles, chin on his paws, watching us as if he understands something is shifting. I roll socks into tight pairs. Label sunscreen with a Sharpie. Tuck flashlights into side pockets.

Camp Kesem—a week for kids who have a parent affected by cancer, or who've lost one. The boys don't know what to expect. Neither do I. My coworker told me her grandson loves it. I cling to that.

Conor's week will include a three day backpacking trip with other kids his age. He's reluctant. Ryan is excited but he wonders what he will be doing.

"Will there be campfires?" he asks.

"I think so," I say, "maybe swimming or water play too. They want us to pack a swimsuit."

We've been told about the support group. We'll get there. At the six-month mark.

We get through Father's Day.

Chapter 24
The Earthquake

It was a quiet evening in 1989. I was at the little house that Tom and Dylan were renting while Tom pursued his master's degree in English literature. He was supposed to have left for a men's fellowship meeting in Richmond, but he'd decided to stay home.

We were sitting at the kitchen table, catching up before he dug into his writing. Dylan was down the block, playing outside with a few neighborhood kids.

Just as Tom got up to attend to the whistling teapot, the floor began to shudder. Living in California, earthquakes usually passed quickly. But this one lingered, and it packed a bigger punch than usual.

"This is a big one," Tom said, moving to the front doorway.

He checked the street for Dylan, making sure he was not alone, and watched the pavement ripple like a wave. I ducked under the table—thin, rickety, offering more comfort than protection.

"Julie, you've got to see this—the street looks like an ocean," he said, motioning for me to join him in the doorway.

I stayed put.

When the shaking stopped, a child's voice split the silence. "Daaaaaad!"

Dylan's cry carried down the block. Tom stepped into the yard just as Dylan rounded the corner, sprinting full speed. He scooped him up mid-run and held him tight.

Later, we walked through downtown, taking in the cracked walls and fallen bricks. When we learned the extent of the damage—the deaths, the collapsed freeways—we were stunned. Tom read about the Cypress Structure collapse and realized how close he would have been if he'd gone to his meeting. He shook his head and said quietly, *"Lucky night to stay home."*

I didn't know then how many times the ground would shift again—or how much I'd miss the steadiness in his voice.

Chapter 25
Empty House

The first few days while the boys are gone pass slowly. I move from room to room without purpose, folding laundry that doesn't need folding. The sun is shining. Birds are singing. I register it all without feeling any of it.

I lie in bed longer than I should. My bladder is full, but not enough to compel me out from under the covers.

By midweek, the quiet feels like a living thing. It's the first time since Tom died that the house has been this still. Without the boys here, I see more clearly what their presence gives me: a reason to get out of bed, to move, to function. Their needs tether me to the living. Without them, it's just me and the ache.

Tomorrow is Tom's birthday.

He'd been making plans for a repeat bicycle ride down the coast from Northern to Southern California—like he and his brother Joe did back when Tom and I were dating. Tom talked about it with that spark in his voice, like he was already halfway there. I hate that he never got to take that trip.

I think about today's training run. Coach Jeff, sensing I needed distraction, swaps my rest day for a short three-miler.

Even that feels ambitious. The idea of changing clothes alone feels exhausting.

I stand in the bedroom holding my running shoes, weighing options that shouldn't require this much effort. Rest. Run. Nothing at all.

The house is immaculate, but not because I've tended to it. It has simply stayed that way. No backpacks slumped against the wall. No shoes left on the living room floor. No cereal bowls abandoned in the sink.

I stand in the kitchen, hand on the counter, and try to remember when it last felt like this. A house without friction. Without demand.

On the table, the roses sag in their vase, their petals darkened and curled, leaves dropping one by one onto the wood. They look exactly like the cover of the book beside them—*A Grief Observed*. I didn't plan that. I just notice it now.

Tomorrow the boys will come home. Tomorrow Tom would have turned fifty.

I leave the roses where they are, petals dropping one by one onto the table.

Chapter 26
The Shoreline

The boys are home. We don't linger in the chaos of unpacking—camp duffels and sleeping bags dropped beside the washing machine—because we have somewhere to go. Tonight, we go to the ocean.

The sand is cool beneath our feet as we walk toward the water—barefoot, quiet, each of us carrying something different. The moon is a waxing gibbous, casting a soft light across the surface of the Pacific. The sky is clear. The ocean is dark and cold, its rhythm steady, endless.

We don't run into the waves tonight—not even the boys. Normally, they'd charge in screaming, all limbs and joy, letting the icy Northern California water wake them from the inside out. But not tonight. Tonight, we move together with purpose. With reverence.

JuLee goes first—Tom's ex-wife, Dylan's mother. I had to ask her to share this place—and to join us. Tom had never shown me. Years ago, she and Tom scattered the ashes of their newborn daughter here. She steps into the surf, lifts the urn, and releases a portion of his ashes into the tide. The wind carries the gray dust for a moment before it drifts into the water. Then she turns and hands the urn to Ryan.

He clutches it tightly with both hands.

"Bye, Dad. I love you," he says, his voice steady and sure. "Tell Grandma and Grandpa hello."

Then my eight-year-old tips the urn carefully, watching the ashes fall into the sea. Tears slip down his cheeks as he turns to Conor and holds out the urn.

Conor steps forward, pulls the urn close, and closes his eyes.

"I will make you proud, Dad. I love you."

The waves lap at his shins. He doesn't flinch. He pours the ashes slowly, deliberately.

Dylan goes next. He speaks with quiet grace—something poetic, heartfelt. I can't remember the exact words now, only the tone. His words warm my heart while the icy water numbs my feet.

Then it's my turn.

Conor and Ryan look over at me. But it's harder than I imagined. I look away, out to the ocean, where the moonlight ripples silver across the waves. The cool plastic of the urn presses against my palms, urging me forward. Still, I hesitate.

I'm not ready to let go of what's left of Tom. Just three months ago, I drove around with this urn seat-belted beside me, talking to him as if he were still beside me. Now I wonder what it will be like once the ashes are gone.

I glance at JuLee. She gives me a reassuring smile, as if she knows what this moment costs me. My words stick in my throat, weighted with the finality of it all.

"I'm not ready to say goodbye, Tom," I manage. "I miss you. I love you."

That's all I can force out. The rest stays locked inside my chest—unspoken but alive.

When the last of his ashes are gone, JuLee hands me a rose—the same gesture she once made with Tom, after they scattered their daughter's ashes here. I step forward and toss it gently into the surf. It floats for a moment, drifts away, then comes back. Conor picks it up and throws it out again. Again, it comes back. One by one, we throw it out—until finally it drifts away.

We stand together in silence, the five of us, watching the waves and the moonlight shimmer across the water. We don't speak. We don't need to. After a bit, we sit on the beach and read a few of Tom's poems. It feels right.

Chapter 27
Something New

It's early fall now, and we're still moving through the same currents—grief, fear, exhaustion. Ryan and I are walking into something new. Together.

We sit in the van outside the hospice where we each will have our support group sessions. Ryan fidgets with the strap on his backpack while I grip the steering wheel, pretending to feel calm. We've been here before—a few times, for one-on-one sessions with the grief counselor. But tonight is different. We're both stepping into group sessions—one for grade school kids and the other for parents of grieving children.

The counselor says we're ready, though I'm not sure what that means.

My chest feels cinched tight, like a corset pulled too far. I force a breath, pull the corners of my mouth up in an attempt to smile at Ryan, and open the door.

The hallway is quiet and softly lit with a few pieces of artwork on the walls. Nothing bright or cheery, but not sterile either. Just warm enough to feel safe. It's the kind of place that knows not to overwhelm you.

"I'm just in the next room," I call to him.

I watch him follow the signs to the kids' group—the room already buzzing like an indoor playground.

The door to my room is wide open. A chill hits me as I peer inside. I pull my sweater around me like a security blanket and step inside. There are a few moms already in the room sitting around a long conference table topped with two battered boxes of tissues. Once again, I attempt to smile, knowing they can see that it is fake.

I close my eyes and take a few deep breaths. Just then, the door bursts open and the kids from the other room flood in— like a hurricane of noise and motion.

"This is a way we ease the children in group sessions here," I hear the facilitator say. I'm not sure if my head or the room is spinning as the kids jump and shout. They seem at ease to me. Even Ryan looks okay—though much less energized.

The first activity is "Emotional Twister."

"Right foot: Fear," the facilitator calls out.

I pick up my right foot and place it on a yellow square. My head throbs and my body tightens as the kids erupt in laughter, a young girl falling onto her side as she reaches for the blue square. I take a few more deep breaths in an effort not to walk out.

After a few chaotic minutes, the kids are ushered back to their room down the hall, the noise fading as the door closes behind them.

We begin with introductions, going around the table one by one. Most of the other moms are returning and already know each other and their stories. I'm one of only two newcomers.

"Hi," I say nervously.

The other moms smile at me.

"My name is Julie. My husband died about six months ago from lung cancer. I have two boys at home—eight and fifteen —and an older stepson who lives in Southern California."

There is more to say, so much more. But for now, we've started.

The facilitator tells us what makes this group different.

"For parents of grieving children, it isn't only about your own grief," the facilitator says. "It's also about caring for your children who are also grieving—and there's no way to separate the two."

She explains that the work here is not about stopping grief. It's about staying present with it—ours and our children's—without letting one eclipse the other. We need space to keep processing our own loss, she says, just as our kids need space for theirs. The danger comes when either of us feels we have to hide it to protect the other. I can see Ryan sometimes doing this for me. I do the same with Conor. And sometimes—without meaning to—I expect Conor to carry on as if nothing has changed, even though everything has.

"But that's not all. Young kids don't go through grief in a linear fashion," she adds. "Children revisit the loss at each stage of development."

She hands out a sheet of paper. On it is a simple chart—stages of childhood development lined up beside how grief might show up as they revisit loss as they grow. Each developmental leap brings new understanding, new questions, new pain. Grief changes shape as they do.

We talk about how hard this is—how we're expected to be steady when we feel anything but. How we're meant to guide our children through something we don't understand ourselves. There is no clean separation between their grief and ours.

I study the paper in my hands and try to imagine what this will mean for Ryan and Conor—and for me. At this point, I'm still focused on surviving the week. I write notes in the margins anyway, fold the paper carefully, and tuck it into my bag.

Conor attends support group too, though his is on a different night from mine and Ryan's. His group is just for teens—other kids who've lost a parent. I don't walk him in. He wouldn't want that. Teens aren't like that. I pull into the parking lot, park the car, and watch him go in on his own. He follows a pretty girl whose family pulled in beside us. I say nothing. It's the first time I've seen a glimmer of interest in anything other than his closed bedroom door.

Afterward, I ask him how it went. He shrugs as he tells me, "It was fine." That's all I get. I focus on the disappointment that he doesn't share more with me. I should be grateful that he's no longer listing reasons not to go.

He doesn't say much to me anymore. I hope—desperately —that he's sharing more in his group than he does at home. Their facilitators use art too, encourage them to work through their emotions with drawing, and then talk about what comes up. I hope he gives it a chance and draws something. Even more, I pray that he shares something.

I don't know what he shares in that room. I only know I have to keep showing up to mine.

Stacks of pastels, color markers, and paper are already spread across the table when I walk in for our second group session. I feel a flicker of excitement, immediately followed by a moment of fear thinking that we might be joined by the kids again.

We begin with more sharing. I reach for the box of tissues as I listen to one gut-wrenching story after another.

When it's my turn, I surprise myself.

"I keep forgetting things," I say.

The words feel small compared to death. Petty even.

"I hear someone's name and it disappears before they finish their sentence. I park my car and then walk up and down the lot trying to find it. There are a lot of green Siennas in parking lots these days."

A few of the moms smile softly.

Heads begin to nod.

One woman says she put milk in the pantry last week.

Another admits she rereads emails three times and still can't remember what they said. Someone else says she once forgot why she drove to the grocery store at all.

The stories start tumbling out.

I hadn't known I needed that.

The facilitator waits until the room quiets again.

"Grief affects memory," she says gently. "Your brains are under strain. You're surviving something enormous. Short-term memory is often the first thing to suffer."

Relief moves through me like a breath I didn't know I was holding.

So I'm not losing my mind.

I'm grieving.

When it's time to draw, I hesitate. I don't know what to put on the page. But as I sit in front of the paper, it comes. I reach for the red pastel and begin drawing a swirl—gently at first, then pressing harder as the anger I've buried deep in my chest lands on the page.

It's a strange exercise that feels like picking at a scab just to watch it bleed. When I speak about it later, I feel distant, like I'm describing someone else's pain. But then, after my turn to share passes, something shifts. What had been buried rises. By the time we leave, I am raw.

Across the table from me sits a mom with a boy and a girl, close to Ryan's age. She's been attending this group for nearly three years. Her husband died when the kids were still very young. And yet, even now, she seems to be drowning in it. Her grief is loud and unfiltered—edged with raw anger. I wonder if I'll still feel this way three years from now. I pray I won't.

The group ends, and once again, we are let out into the world—to fend for ourselves and our children for another week. Two sessions in, and I'm beginning to understand: healing doesn't happen in the room. It happens in the days that follow.

Chapter 28
Chicago

I stand at the start line of the Chicago Marathon.

Tom and I chose this race together.

I'm here without him.

Around me, 45,000 runners stretch and bounce in the unseasonable heat. The air smells like sunscreen, sweat, and nervous adrenaline. Conor, Ryan, Dylan, and several Chicago-based cousins will be waiting at the finish.

It's been a brutal few months. Next week, I begin again at a new job. Ryan, just eight, curls into "Dad's spot" every night —afraid he won't wake up. His hand grips mine in the dark. He's already faced too much death: first Papa B, my stepdad, gone to cancer a year and a half before Tom. Now his dad.

Conor tries to act tough, but grief eats away at him in ways I don't see until it breaks through the cracks. He's fourteen, still a boy, trying to protect his brother and me from a world that no longer feels safe.

I close my eyes, trying to keep the tears back. My throat tightens as the grief presses in. Then, a memory surfaces— Tom and my first ride down Highway 1. Maybe a date. Maybe not.

We meet at the local grocery store, where I'm bagging

groceries after track practice my senior year of high school. Tom is smart, dry-humored, carrying a quiet sadness behind his eyes that makes me want to know him more.

We know each other for a couple years before he calls out across the store: "Hey, Calvo. You run a lot. Do you have a bike?"

He's always called me by Calvo—my last name.

I blink. "Yeah. Why?"

He grins. "I'm riding down the coast. Want to come?"

I shrug like it's no big deal, but my heart leaps. I don't know if he sees me as a friend or something more. I just show up.

That morning, he unloads our bikes from his truck, pops in his headphones, and rides off without a word. I watch him disappear around a bend, fast and lean. "Okay, not a date," I mutter. I jump on my bike and try to chase him down.

My legs burn, lungs ache, but I catch him eventually. He waits on the shoulder, grinning. We prop our bikes together and walk down to the beach. The air smells of salt and kelp. Seagulls screech overhead. A fishing boat bobs far offshore. We sit on the sand, quiet, watching the waves. The silence feels charged. I don't know what this is. I only know I want to stay.

Later, we climb over some rocks where the waves crash. He calls for me to come out to the edge. I hang back, nervous. He sits, shirtless on the rocks, freckled skin glistening. Then—a huge wave explodes against the rocks, drenching him. His nylon shorts cling tight, leaving nothing to the imagination. I double over laughing, breathless. Date or no date, I've never felt more alive.

BANG!

The starting gun cracks, and I snap back to the race. We surge forward like a tide.

Chicago swelters. The heat presses in from every direction. Sweat drips down my spine, soaks my singlet, pools in my shoes. I start slow and steady—no chance for a Boston Qualifier today. Maybe I can just keep going.

Crowds line the course, shouting encouragement. Their voices blend into a roar. Some hold hoses, spraying arcs of cool water across the street. I run through one, grateful for the relief. It blasts my skin and revives me for a moment. Still, the heat wears on me. My singlet clings heavy with sweat, the fabric chafing under my arms.

Every step feels like pushing the jogging stroller uphill after Ryan got heavier—leaning into it, legs straining, wheels fighting me. My body begs me to stop.

The boys plan to meet me at the halfway mark, but as I pass mile 13, I don't see them. I scan the sidewalks, heart lifting and sinking with each face. Nothing. I start to worry about all of them waiting in the extreme heat. A mile later, I call. A train broke down earlier, and theirs was delayed. They've gone straight to the finish line. I tell them, "Just head back to the hotel. It's too hot."

At mile 22, about three and a half hours in, a voice blares through loudspeakers overhead: "THE RACE IS NOW CLOSED. Proceed to the nearest aid station for transport to the finish."

I hear gasps around me. One runner has died. Dozens are down. The heat is merciless.

A line of buses stretches down the block, but the line of runners extends for several more. There are murmurs that we'll get out of the heat faster if we just walk to the finish rather than waiting. I keep going. It's faster than waiting. My vision blurs as sweat stings my eyes. I wipe it away and let my mind drift again.

I hear his voice: I love you.

The last time.

His eyes—ocean blue, heavy with goodbye—lock with mine.

We know our future is slipping away.

A helicopter thumps overhead.

"STOP RUNNING," the loudspeaker commands the thousands of runners still on the course. "FOR YOUR OWN SAFETY, WALK."

The tone is harsh, dystopian. It feels like I'm in a disaster film. I slow to a walk, but walking hurts more than shuffling. My legs cramp, my hips scream, but I keep moving.

The helicopter skims past, its shadow flickering across the pavement. A gentle spray from a spectator's hose drifts across the street and hits me in the face. The heat rises off the asphalt and my legs churn toward the finish.

After nearly a mile of trudging, I break into a slow jog. I hear the finish line now—the echo of cheers, the static crackle of the loudspeaker. I crest the final hill at mile 26—the finish comes into view. The clock is still running. Volunteers wait at the line.

I cross the finish line. A volunteer places a medal around my neck. I am too tired to cry.

Chapter 29
Seventeen Years

It would've been our seventeenth wedding anniversary.

I drive the boys to school like any other Friday. I could say something. I don't.

I park and walk Ryan to morning daycare at his school. I sign him in as he shrugs off his backpack and runs toward the other kids without hesitation. He likes it there—the leaders, the noise, the safety of routine. I watch him for a moment longer than usual before turning away.

Conor's classes start earlier than Ryan's. I join the lineup of cars dropping students off a block from campus, just before the stoplight where the student drivers turn in. He crosses the street without looking back. I wait until he reaches the sidewalk, then turn the corner and head home.

By mid-morning, I drive to the running store. It's quiet—just Tim unpacking a shipment of apparel, two large cardboard boxes split open near the women's section.

"Hey, Julie," he says, looking up. "Time for a new pair already?"

I nod. He disappears into the back and returns with my usual model before I even ask.

I try them on, jog a few steps across the worn carpet. The

cushioning feels alive again—springy in a way my old pair hasn't in weeks.

My therapist told me to be kind to myself on days like this. Buying the shoes feels like a start.

When I get home, I lace up the new shoes and go for a run. It's cool out. The late-winter light is soft and slanted, the air crisp in my lungs. The new shoes push back against the pavement. I hadn't realized how flat my old pair had become until now. I let my body lead, breath finding rhythm, feet striking pavement, thoughts loosening.

Later, I walk the aisles of the grocery store with quiet focus: ground beef, ricotta, crushed tomatoes, mozzarella, garlic bread, greens, cabernet. I reach automatically for the ricotta he always bought—the full-fat kind, never part-skim. He said it made the layers hold. Tom's lasagna dinner. His family's recipe—though he seemed to be the only one of the six siblings who ever made it. It was his thing. He cooked it for birthdays, special occasions.

This year, I want to stay in. To fill our kitchen with his memory.

The kitchen is small—just enough space to turn and reach. I brown the meat slowly, stirring the sauce like he used to. There's a calm in the ritual. A quiet kind of reverence.

As I cook, memories rise—not just of our wedding, but everything that came before it. I stir the sauce as it thickens, the spoon dragging slow circles through the pot.

We married in that small flat in San Francisco, already expecting Conor. Not long after, we moved back to my childhood neighborhood, thinking proximity would make new parenthood easier. It was harder than we expected. We kept going. We made it sixteen years.

By the time the lasagna is cooling and the wine is breathing, the boys come home. The smell of garlic and sauce pulls them into the kitchen.

"Lasagna?" Ryan asks.

"It would've been our anniversary today," I tell them, pouring a glass of cabernet. "Seventeen years."

They don't say much, but they understand. That's all I need.

We eat together. They go back for seconds. I sip the wine he used to love. The candle flickers low.

Later, after the dishwasher hums and the house quiets, I sit alone with a second glass and think of that balloon floating above the farmland. The smile he gave me when he said, "I guess we won't be needing these today," holding up the bungee cords we'd each packed in secret.

I raise my glass toward the empty chair.

"Happy anniversary," I whisper. "I still do."

Then I blow out the candle, rinse my glass, and turn off the lights.

Chapter 30
MacGyvering

When I was growing up, he was Jim. He married my mom when I was a tween and stepped into our family with a kind of steadiness I hadn't known before. He was careful never to take my dad's place, but he filled so many of the gaps my parents left. Later, when my boys came along, he became Papa B. In my mind, giving him "Papa" somehow helped offset the fact that I never called him Dad.

We honored him in other ways too. Conor carries his name as his middle name—Conor James. A small reminder that even if I couldn't call him Dad, he was still woven into the fabric of our family.

What I remember most, though, aren't the big gestures. It's the everyday moments that showed his care. Like the afternoons in the garage, where I'd hover nearby while he worked. I liked being there, watching his hands move, listening to him think out loud as he tinkered with whatever was broken that week.

In the garage, I leaned against his workbench, watching him fiddle with some half-repaired gadget. He had a coffee tin full of random screws, springs, and wires, all of them laid out like puzzle pieces waiting for their place.

"Go grab me some aluminum foil," he said, gesturing toward the kitchen.

I darted inside, pulling the roll from the cabinet, and came back. As he tore off a strip, we laughed about how MacGyver on TV could fix anything with just a gum wrapper. Jim explained why foil was better—more permanent, less chance of a fire. He always explained. He never brushed me off as "just a kid." He wanted me to understand.

Years later, after Tom dies, I find myself in that same kind of silence—with a broken house and a broken life. I don't feel safe letting strangers into the house, and money was tight anyway. I wish Papa were still around—not just to fix things, but to steady me the way he always did.

Sometimes my brother in Sacramento fills the gap, talking me through a clogged sink or a blown fuse over the phone. Once, when the bathroom sink kept backing up no matter what I tried, he came down with a snake and fed it into the drain. When he pulled it back out, a dense knot of hair and soap and who-knows-what came with it. More than I expected. More than seemed possible.

He didn't comment on it. Just dropped the mess into a trash bag and rinsed the tool clean.

Neither of us said what we were both thinking.

Often it was just me, tools spread across the counter, heart racing as I try to figure it out.

When the sink backs up or the fuse blows, I hear his voice —slow down, look at it, don't panic. And when it comes to the boys, I do the same.

I can still see him there in the garage, the window over the workbench casting a dull light across the clutter he refused to throw away—coffee tins of screws, bent springs, scraps of wire waiting for their next purpose. He never saw broken as final. Just unfinished.

Chapter 31
Thanksgiving

The house smells like rosemary, garlic, and roasted turkey. My sisters and newly married brother arrive with their spouses and kids, each carrying foil-covered casseroles or store-bought pies. For the first time, we are hosting the extended family for Thanksgiving.

In some ways, it is easier this way—less disruption, less pretending—but harder, too. Every room holds echoes of the unfulfilled promise we saw when we moved into this house less than four years ago.

I keep flashing back to the year before. We'd been at my sister Carol's house, as usual. Tom had only had two glasses of wine—well under what would normally affect him—but something wasn't right. His words slurred. His movements lagged as if he were drunk. I assumed he must have had more than I realized. I was angry—furious.

The fear from that DUI years earlier, when I was pregnant with Conor, never quite left me.

The day after Thanksgiving at Carol's, I told Tom that I wouldn't live like that—not with someone who drank too much, and especially not with someone who might drink and drive again. He didn't argue. He quit cold turkey.

For a while, he slept on the couch, saying he needed space from anything that might make him want to drink. I told myself it was temporary, that giving him room was a kind of love. But every night, the glow of the TV downstairs reminded me how far apart we'd drifted. When the shoulder pain began, he came back to bed. He said the couch was wrecking his back, but I think it was already something deeper. I remember lying on the very edge of the bed, afraid to move or breathe too loudly, as if stillness could keep the peace between us.

Looking back, it wasn't the wine. It was the tumors—four of them—already pressing on the parts of his brain that controlled speech, balance, impulse. By March, they'd cause strokes. Even that Thanksgiving, they must have been there, hiding in the dark.

Now, I am hosting. I spread a tablecloth over the outdoor table. Carol brings her folding table and a few collapsible chairs to help us make room. Conor and Ryan run back and forth helping set up while cousins spill into the hallway. Everyone brings something, making the day possible.

Dylan gives Conor a remote-controlled fart machine. We slip it into my brother Robert's back pocket and send him to make small talk with our sister Linda. The boys hide around the corner, triggering the sound effects at the worst possible moment. Robert plays along, excusing himself and apologizing for his untimely release. We watch Linda's face twist in shock, then confusion and disgust. When she finally catches on, the whole room dissolves into laughter. It was the first true, unstoppable laughter I'd heard in the house in months.

After everyone leaves, the house feels both overstuffed and hollow. I sit alone at the kitchen table, the air still warm from too many bodies, too many stories.

My family has filled the house. Laughter too. This year, I don't ask for more.

Chapter 32
In The Holiday Fog

The little gifts pile up on my desk—wrapped soaps, tins of cookies, peppermint lotion. My coworkers drop them off with cheerful smiles, and I smile back, wishing I had something to place in their hands too. I want to, I mean to, but my thoughts keep slipping.

For the moms in my grief group, I imagine journals— something that might help them shape their own words. I walk the aisles of the gift shop, pick some up, put them down. The covers aren't right, the paper feels cheap, nothing seems worthy. I spend too long searching, second-guessing every choice, and in the end, I talk myself out of it completely.

When our last session before the holiday arrives, the others bring candles, teas, ornaments. Their gifts look small but whole—gestures of thoughtfulness. I bring nothing but good intentions, my empty hands folded in my lap.

During the session, our counselor suggests writing letters to the person we've lost—slipping them into a stocking or memory box each year, or just the years we feel like it. The boys aren't interested, so I write my own—words I can't say out loud, folded and tucked into Tom's stocking above the fireplace.

Dearest love, I write. *I miss you. I don't know how I can go on without you holding my hand, but I will. I promise you that I will raise our kids as best as I am able, whatever that's worth. Please send me hellos from heaven.*

It isn't much, but it is something.

We already have Lucky, our black Lab, but I think maybe another dog will help—especially for Conor, who's been drifting away from the family. A couple of days before Christmas, he finds a two-year-old yellow lab named Chaz online. The following day, we head to the Humane Society, wait three hours, and finally meet Chaz—known to the staff as "Chaz the Spaz." Seconds into the visit, he jumps and nearly catches my eye with a toenail. I leave his kennel with a black eye and a firm no.

The long wait gives us time to walk the kennels and check out two other dogs. We spot a black one we somehow haven't seen—ten months old, eighty pounds, deep brown eyes, and a calm beneath the puppy energy. His name is Ronin, which means masterless warrior. We'll be his fourth owner. The name is a little too fitting.

We bring him home on Christmas Eve.

Just before dinner, Dylan arrives. Lucky and Ronin go outside, and Ronin comes back with poop smeared on the long fur of his hind legs, tracking it through the house. Dylan snaps, assuming I brought home a full-grown dog that isn't house-trained. Ryan jumps in, telling him he's still a puppy. Dylan looks over at me for confirmation. I nod and grab scissors, trimming the fur on Ronin's hind legs before reapplying my makeup to cover the shadow from Chaz's parting gift.

That night, the boys and I wrap gifts and bake chocolate chip cookies for Santa. In the morning, the tree is still lit, the presents have multiplied, and white paw prints lead from the fireplace to the deck, where chewed carrot tops scatter in the cold. The milk glass is nearly empty, clouded with soggy cookie crumbs—proof enough for Ryan that Santa is real.

The stockings bulge with candy, cuties, Pringles, and tooth-brushes.

Beside Tom's stocking is the small wrapped box: Two Boogers & a Box of Rocks. It began as a joke. Tom used to tease the boys that if they weren't good, they'd get nothing but "two boogers and a box of rocks" for Christmas. The last Christmas before he got sick, we decided to make it real. We wrapped a small box filled with tiny rocks, then added two booger-sized blobs of adhesive dots from my scrapbooking supplies. On top we placed a tag that read, Two Boogers & a Box of Rocks, and tucked it into Tom's stocking. The boys laughed out loud when he pulled it out, and Tom played along, roaring, "What. Is. THIS?"

Now the box sits beside his stocking again, a joke turned tradition. For a few hours, with Dylan home, the four of us feel almost whole.

Two days after Christmas, it's my birthday—December 27. It always gets lost in the holidays. The boys make me bacon and eggs—sweet, careful, thoughtful—but by mid-morning they've drifted into their own worlds. The house falls quiet. The warmth of breakfast fades into a hush that feels like the days after the funeral, when the visitors were gone and only the ache remained. My birthday has always carried that risk—sliding into the shadows of Christmas—but this year the emptiness hits harder without Tom to notice it, to make it matter.

A few days later, Ryan and I visit Dottie, our old neighbor with a December 31 birthday. She understands what it means to share a birthday with the holidays—the way it can vanish beneath the glitter and noise. Her small living room smells of coffee and birthday cake, a celebration squeezed into the year's final hours.

Ryan, wide-eyed, tells her about the paw prints, the uneaten carrot tops, the cookie crumbs in the milk.

"Mom hates dunking cookies," he explains. "So the kids at school are wrong. It can't be our parents."

Dottie smiles and lets him have his wonder, and so do I.

Hitting the Wall
Breaking Open

Chapter 33
Fractured

The crutches announce me before I enter the room—rubber tips thudding, uneven, louder than they should be. My armpits are already sore, rubbed raw from the awkward pressure of holding myself upright. Every doorway feels narrower than it used to be.

By January fifteenth, I'm on them full-time. A fractured metatarsal—one of those tiny bones you never think about until it refuses to carry you.

I hate the crutches almost immediately. They're exhausting in a way that has nothing to do with fitness and everything to do with imbalance. I feel clumsy, dependent, unwieldy. After a few days, my doctor gives me the option to switch to a boot. It costs more, but it frees my hands. I limp around with an uneven gait, grateful at least to be moving under my own power.

At work, I keep a cooler of ice water under my desk, soaking my foot until it goes numb. I tell myself this is temporary. I tell myself I can endure anything if it's moving somewhere.

Stillness is more exhausting than motion. I'm used to fixing things.

With nowhere to go and nothing to burn off the hours, I start opening drawers I haven't touched since Tom died.

Weekends and evenings are spent stuck at home with my foot submerged in ice. To pass the time, I start pulling out old pieces of Tom's writing—essays, journal entries, poems he read aloud again and again. Back then, I'd struggle to stay with the thread, the complexity. I'd urge him to break them into smaller, easier chunks. I thought maybe he'd find more readers if his poems weren't so long.

He shared his writing online and watched quietly to see who would come. Not many did.

After some begging, I let Ryan create a blog as well. I figured it could be a fun way for him to practice writing over the summer. He wrote about summer camp, Pokémon cards, and even the day he got hit in the head with a rock and needed stitches. Like Tom, Ryan didn't love that his only readers were Mom and Dad. He wanted to know why I had so many. So I explained the blogosphere's unspoken rule of reciprocal support and let him leave comments on some of my favorite running blogs.

One day, Ryan overheard his dad complaining about how few readers he was seeing in the stats.

"You have to comment on the other blogger's writing and they will come read your writing and even leave a comment," Ryan explained.

"I'm not going to do that," Tom said flatly.

"Well… that's what I did, and I had 22 readers and 5 new comments," Ryan said proudly.

Tom just grumbled. I gave Ryan a small shrug.

Tom didn't take my feedback well either. His writing was something he held close, almost tender in the way he guarded it.

He wrote about death—almost always death. We used to joke that his blog was "the death blog." It wasn't really funny.

From the moment I met him, he was already grieving. I thought, stupidly, that maybe I could love him back to life.

But grief doesn't work like that. You can't mend someone else's pain. You can only sit beside it.

Now that he's gone, I read his work differently. I catch the hidden layers, the symbolism and small shifts in phrasing that used to frustrate me. His words were never just about what they said. He was giving shape to what stayed lodged inside him.

I wonder now if I had listened beyond the structure and length—if I had heard the grief underneath the craft—would I have understood more of what he carried? I'm not sure I could have. Loving someone doesn't mean you understand everything they carry.

When we were first falling in love, he once wrote a piece shorter than most of his later work. He read it to me on Easter Sunday, 1986, when I met him at a park during his lunch break from the grocery store where we both worked. It was hot for early spring. The sun made me squint as I crossed the park toward him. He was finishing a cigarette when I walked up, smoke curling around him in the heat. I kissed him anyway. By then I was used to the taste—that faint bitterness mingled with something sweeter. I remember sweat slipping down the center of my back as he read from a yellow legal pad, his handwriting slanted and urgent.

These were my favorite lines:

Her eyes are green with hints of brown,
and her skin is brown and soft and smooth to the touch...
Her eyes, her eyes, her eyes.
How can I possibly describe those beautiful eyes.

Back then, I thought it was beautiful. I still do—grand and poetic in that young, passionate way. The piece wasn't only about me. Even then, he was writing love alongside something heavier. Now I read it and feel the urgency under the words. He was trying to pin a fleeting moment to the page. To believe love could hold off death.

After he died, I found more of his writing. Not all of it was flattering. He wrote about me—my jealousy, my insecurities. I could hear his frustration. I could also hear how hard he was trying to understand me. Some of those pages I kept. Some I read twice, three times, trying to decide whether they were truth or just frustration caught in ink. I held them longer than I meant to. In the end, I tore a few in half and dropped them into the trash. I couldn't bear the weight of them. What remains is tucked away.

The rubber sole thuds against the kitchen tile. The weeks crawl.

February arrives and the first anniversary edges closer. I'm still trying to live a life that doesn't include him. My children keep me busy; they give me purpose—sometimes too much. But the helplessness still loops and loops.

Little by little, I'm walking again. Four weeks in the boot, then a gradual return to motion. But not running—not yet. I defer my race entry for Napa until the following year. It feels like defeat, but also relief. When I do run it, there will be a lot of memories to face.

Instead of running, I find another outlet. In the garage, Conor's punching bag hangs from the ceiling, swaying slightly in the drafty dark. I start hitting it. No gloves—just bare fists until my knuckles sting and my breath is hard and fast.

I don't know if I'm mad at the universe, at cancer, at Tom for leaving me, or at myself for still not being able to keep everything together. I just know I have to hit something.

Chapter 34
Falling Apart

On the drive home, the tears come without warning. Not quiet tears—the kind that claw from your gut and sit like a weight behind your eyes until they finally break free. I cry the whole way home.

As February turns toward March, the dates begin to line up with the year before. February 28—the stroke.

The night before, I wake from a dream where it is happening again. Not a vague dream, but the memory itself. His body faltering. My voice calling his name. I jolt upright in the dark, panic flooding my chest before I remember where I am. Before I remember this already happened.

The days that follow arrive in order. Not because I call them up, but because they come for me. A Bob Dylan song in a coffee shop and I'm back in our family room—the hospital bed near the fireplace, flames moving behind the grate. The rocking chair in pieces beside it—slats separated, the carved back detached, the curved runners lying apart. Sometimes it's a date. Sometimes it's a sound. Sometimes it's nothing I can name at all.

I'm not trying to remember. The memories find me.

These past weeks feel like reliving Tom's death in slow motion—this time without an end point.

Before, I watched my husband's life slip away. Now it feels like I'm watching my son unravel, piece by piece—and I don't know how to stop it.

Conor tells me he wants to quit baseball. He doesn't enjoy it anymore.

"I don't enjoy anything anymore," he says.

I know exactly what he means.

I pray his coach will talk him out of quitting. I pray he'll hold on a little longer—stay connected to something. I know it won't change what's underneath, but I still want him to try. I want him to care.

When I call him from the house phone, he asks why I'm home. He's forgotten that Ryan and I had group today. Without thinking, I tell him I didn't like my job anymore… so I quit.

Silence.

"I love you," he says.

The truth is, I'd rushed home to gather the coffee mugs Tom collected from every dot-com job he worked. My plan is to hurl them against the fence. Let them shatter. Let something break besides me.

I don't follow through—not yet. I place them gently on the table outside and go upstairs for a hot shower. It's all I can manage in that moment.

In the shower, I begin pulling clumps of hair from the drain. It's been happening for months now. Not stray strands —clumps I gather in my palm before the water backs up. Later, the brush fills quickly. The sink gathers more. My hair has always been thick, so no one comments. But I see it.

People keep saying, "You should do something for yourself."

My idea of self-care is a run.

A friend put it differently. He says that to take care of myself, I have to represent myself the best I can—not escape, but show up. For me, that meant showing up as a parent. Standing up for Conor, even when I don't agree with how he treats his teachers. Asking them to work with me. Wanting them to understand—without spelling it out—that grief makes everything harder.

Later that day, I go back outside. The mugs are still there—their handles chipped, a few logos fading. I pick one up, then another. This time, I don't hesitate.

I hurl them against the brick chimney. One after another. Sharp, satisfying bursts, shards scattering across the concrete like tiny pieces of a language I can't speak any other way. The release doesn't erase my anger, but it loosens something inside me.

I save a couple of the mugs for Conor and offer him the chance to throw them too. He doesn't take me up on it.

Meanwhile, I keep asking for help—for Conor, for myself. My voice grows louder. The responses thin. Emails to the school go unanswered. Therapists don't call back.

Until they do.

My doctor calls and tells me she knows exactly the right person for Conor. She passes along my information. I book an appointment immediately. Later that same day, his pediatrician calls too. He agrees with the referral. The doctors all seem to concur: this isn't just defiance. It's grief. It's depression.

We're getting somewhere. I think.

That night, I try not to call Conor every fifteen minutes. Last weekend had been that bad. So Ryan and I play Monopoly. We laugh. We watch *Friday Night Lights*. Conor comes home on time.

The next morning, I drive the boys to the dentist in our old town. I let Conor hang out with his friends afterward. Before he leaves, I tell him I love him. That I'm worried. That

I found a therapist who surfs and might actually be pretty cool.

"Okay," he says.

Those weeks blur together—missed calls, crumpled notes from school, the glow of my phone in the dark.

But hard times make you notice the good: a returned call, a smile, the quiet way a teenager says "Okay" and means something softer than surrender. Maybe even trust.

Underneath it all, my worry about Conor intensifies.

The first time he came home reeking of pot, his eyes red, he waved off my concern.

"It's just pot, Ma. Just one time."

I almost believe him. Then the signs stack up. Then a pill tucked away in his room.

When my iPod disappears—the one with Tom's photo under the clear case—I know he doesn't care if I notice anymore. Then comes the black eye. He said it was nothing. I knew better.

He stops answering his phone. Starts slipping out at night.

I'm out of options. And terrified of losing him the way I'd lost Tom.

People tell me to parent harder. Take away everything. Force him to care.

But the truth is gentler, and more complicated. He's my son. I know his heart, even when it's buried under anger and grief. If I strip everything away, I lose whatever fragile thread still connects us. I can't take away the last remaining reasons he might want to get out of bed.

I stop measuring myself against anyone else's way.

I walk an impossible line—firm but not cruel, protective but not smothering, present even when I feel like I'm disappearing.

It isn't about parenting harder.

It's about parenting through grief.

Chapter 35
A Tiny Rose

Years earlier.

I walked to my car after a long day—morning classes at the community college followed by a shift at the grocery store. My legs ached from standing at the register for hours. I pulled the black bowtie from my collar and unbuttoned the top button to let my skin breathe. After the air-conditioned store, the late afternoon heat pressed hard against my face.

The day wasn't over. When I got home, I'd have to return to a Romeo and Juliet paper—pages of half-formed ideas I couldn't quite make sense of, language and symbolism just out of reach.

When I reached my car, I climbed inside and closed the door behind me. The air was warm and thick. I sank into the driver's seat and let out a long breath, relieved to be still for a moment.

Then I saw it—a tiny rose tucked beneath the driver's side wiper, a square of paper folded small around its stem.

The note read, "HELP ME! I need water," followed by a small heart and a "T."

I smiled.

The rose was barely there—small enough to hold between my fingers. I set it on the dashboard just above the steering wheel and went back to the little note, the small square of paper between my fingers. I let myself stay there a moment longer before starting the car.

Chapter 36
Out the Window

I may never know the full extent of Conor's unraveling.

I know he smoked pot. I know he smoked cigarettes—even after watching his father die of lung cancer. I find pills in his room one day, tucked inside a sock in the back of a drawer. But most of the evidence was gone before I can see it—swallowed, smoked, flushed. Hidden.

What I did see was enough.

There's a vacancy in his eyes. A slackness in his expression. His body moves like it belongs to someone else—slower, heavier, indifferent. He stops looking at me. He stops caring whether I see him come or go. Sometimes he doesn't use the front door at all—just climbs out the bedroom window, comes back late, never says where he's been.

I am afraid for his life.

I start thinking about what else I can do—what help even looks like now. I talk with Joe and Kathy, half-formed ideas spilling out between us. Maybe a program—one of those places where you send your kid away. Even thinking it, it feels wrong. Maybe family. I don't know who could take him. Every option feels like failure, but doing nothing feels worse.

Every instinct in me wants to fix it, to smooth things over, but this time fixing means letting go.

In addition to grief support groups, Conor sees a counselor separately for substance use. I try everything I can think of. Still, I feel like I'm losing him.

Part of me is lost too.

Grief lives close to the surface. It doesn't take much to set it off. I smell cigarette smoke in a parking lot and feel a hot surge rise in my chest—not annoyance, but rage. Like a volcano about to erupt.

It's been fifteen years since Tom quit smoking, and it didn't save him. Lung cancer came for him anyway.

It wasn't fair.

I see old men and women still puffing away, somehow untouched. Why Tom? I ask. Why not them?

I'm angry at the doctor who gave us hope—told us Tom had a year. I had braced for three to six months, maybe less. But this doctor told us twelve, and we believed him. We told the boys we had time. That we'd make memories. That we'd be together for one more year. Two weeks later, Tom was gone.

I feel robbed—of time, of truth, of the chance to prepare my kids. I feel guilty too. Guilty for the nights I wanted it to be over, when I couldn't bear to watch him suffer another second.

Part of me feels diminished, harder to reach. Now, six months later, all I want is to feel alive again.

After a run, I collapse on the grass in my front yard and let the thoughts swirl. If Papa were still alive, it might be different. He'd be here—steady and sure—helping me carry the weight. Not to replace Tom, but to give the boys something to lean against. Joe is willing to take Conor in for a while, but he travels often, and with two young kids of his own, it doesn't feel right. I don't know what else to do. I just know something has to change.

Chapter 37
Grief Upon Grief

Word gets to Tom's older brother that I'm struggling with Conor. He reaches out, offering to take him for a while—to give him structure, space, a reset. His assistant emails me with the enrollment forms for the new school. I sign over legal guardianship, with agreement that Conor will come home for visits. He asks that I not come to Hawaii; he worries my presence would blur the lines of who's in charge.

Just days before the one-year mark of Tom's death, I send Conor away.

On the morning of his departure, Ryan clings to Conor's legs, sobbing. "Don't go," he begs. Both boys are crying. Dylan, who is here to accompany Conor to Hawaii, scoops Ryan up in his arms while I step forward. I wrap my arms around Conor, but his body stiffens, cold. He lets me in for a second, then pushes me away, building another layer of distance before he's gone.

Tears blur my eyes as I watch the car pull away. My chest caves in on itself. The house is suddenly quieter, emptier.

Moments later, my phone buzzes.

I can't believe you're doing this.

I HATE YOU!

I sink into the silence, the words burning into me.

When he was a baby, he slept in a small wooden cradle beside our bed. I placed it on the floor, on my side, so I could hear every breath. If I woke in the night and didn't hear him, all I had to do was roll onto my side and look down, reassured by the rise and fall of his chest. When he fussed, I'd reach my hand down to rock the cradle gently, hoping he'd settle with that small movement. Back then, I always knew he was safe.

Now, I can't lean over to see his chest rise, can't reach down and soothe him with my hand. He isn't talking to me, so I have to wait—patient, anxious—for updates.

The helplessness is new.

In the days after, the fear doesn't leave with his departure. When he was here, I would search for him—grab my keys and drive through the neighborhoods that scared me most. My stomach would knot up as I crept past dim parking lots, shadowed street corners, and houses with sagging porches and barred-up windows. A lone kid riding a skateboard would make my pulse spike—until I saw it wasn't Conor. But I always felt relief when I found him, even if it came with a price—the sight of him alive, whole, knuckles bloodied or eyes glassy. Anger and gratitude tangled together in my chest each time I found him.

Now there is no searching. An ocean stretches between us. I wait for updates instead of hunting them down.

At first, the distance only makes the anger louder.

Mean texts flash across my phone, his rage spilling out: cruel words, accusations, reminders that he blames me.

Then—silence. The quiet is worse than the words.

———

Eventually, relief slips in.

I don't have to grab my keys and drive into dangerous neighborhoods that make my skin crawl, easing down unfamiliar streets, my minivan moving too slowly, my shoulders tight. I used to look for his build first—his shape, his gait—because faces blur at that distance. I was careful not to stare too long; I don't want to draw attention from the wrong people. I hate the relief, but it's there all the same.

The house is quieter. Less clutter. Less laundry. More leftovers. I was still learning to cook for three after Tom died; now there are only two. I scrape food into the trash, wrap half-full containers in foil, slide them into the fridge. The silence presses in, like weighted air.

When Ryan goes to his friend's house, the quiet deepens. I wander from room to room, straighten things that don't need straightening. Watching. Worrying. Tracking. It had kept me anchored. Without it, I don't know where to put myself. You can't always run—you have to stop eventually—and stopping means feeling everything without the rhythm that keeps it from overwhelming me.

Relief and guilt sit side by side. Sending Conor away had saved us both, maybe, but it doesn't feel like saving. I promised Tom I'd take care of the boys. Now one of them is being raised by someone else.

I go into Conor's room. I lie down on his bed and cry.

Chapter 38
One Year Gone

One year after Tom's death, I'm lying face-down on a massage table, trying to relax.

In the quiet of the room, I hear Tom. The masseuse glides her hands along my back, pausing when her fingers find the tightness I carry in my shoulders, the places that never truly release. Her hands are warm and deliberate, but it's Tom's presence that steadies me—like sunlight pressing through a closed window.

We communicate, he and I. I ask him what he thinks about my decision to send Conor away—to let him go live with his aunt and uncle in Hawaii. The question tightens my chest. I brace for disappointment. But it doesn't come. His voice is calm. Kind. He reminds me how much he had believed in the importance of a male figure at that age— something he had stressed to me often, even as Conor pushed back on both of us. I felt that resistance more.

I never imagined I'd send my firstborn to live somewhere else. Conor—the baby who cracked open my heart, who showed me the depth of love I didn't know I had. The masseuse's fingers press into the knots at the base of my neck.

I flinch, breathe deep, and remember the moment I first saw him.

His one ear was smooshed from hours pressed against my pubic bone. After forty-seven hours of labor and three hours of pushing, the instant he was in my arms, my heart felt three sizes bigger. Nothing else mattered—not the stalled labor, not the epidural that left me numb and unable to move.

When Patty, one of the nurses from the birth center, called from the birthing center, her voice was warm.

"Hi Momma," she said, "I hear that Conor finally came out to join us."

I stared at my son, beaming.

"He's beautiful, Patty. The most beautiful baby in the world. And I know, because I've seen a lot of babies."

I tried so hard to hold onto that boy. I set boundaries, grounded him, found counseling and tutoring, talked about drugs and alcohol. I even brought home a new puppy. But he told me, "I can't stand to be here. I see Dad dying everywhere I look." And so, fearing I'd lose my son along with my husband if I didn't act, I sent him to Hawaii. He hated me for it, texting: *Fuck you, Mom!*

The masseuse's hands move slowly down my arms, bringing me back to the table, to the quiet room where Tom's presence still feels near.

In the months before I sent him away, my body began to signal what my mind tried to deny. Chest pains would tighten around my sternum without warning, squeezing like a vise. I'd wake in the night convinced I was next—that maybe the boys would lose me, too.

The tests came back mostly fine. A slightly leaking heart valve, they said. "Within normal limits."

Nothing about me felt normal.

I saw a therapist, one-on-one, in addition to grief groups. She told me this kind of grief—sudden, traumatic—would take longer. A year or more of feeling unmoored. I didn't argue. I didn't have the strength to.

I tried Prozac. Wanted it to help. But it dulled everything —my urgency, my focus. I had a teenage son using drugs, slipping out at night, lying to my face. I couldn't afford numbness. Apathy was more dangerous than sadness.

In my journal, I tried to tell the truth: raising a teenager is hard work, and grief makes it nearly impossible. Ten months after Tom's death, I realized how my sorrow had spilled over onto Conor—how I might have been hurting him despite trying so hard to help.

After I sent him away, I held Ryan close. Too close, maybe. I stopped running because I needed him within reach. The dishes piled up; the house sagged under the weight of everything I couldn't face.

Eventually, I found a rhythm at the gym. Ryan sat in the café with his homework while I ran. I always chose a treadmill where we could spot each other easily—a small wave, a quick appearance at the end of the row if he needed me. I ran, but my eyes kept finding him. It was the only way I knew how to breathe.

Ryan also began seeing a therapist—the surfer who rode his bike to work. Ryan called him Dr. Games. He opened up —talking about his dad's death, Conor being sent away, his fear of dying, and frustrations at school. He laughed more. It wasn't a cure, but it was a start.

I kept trying to reach Conor. Small texts, little updates about Ryan, reminders that I love him. Most went unanswered. Somehow the silence felt easier than another *fuck you* in reply—like a quiet, undocumented softening.

A few weeks later, Ryan and I started writing letters. He decorated his with drawings; I filled mine with hope. We received occasional updates—about grades, chores, attitude. None of it sounded good, but I held onto hope that progress would show itself in time.

The masseuse steps out, her soft footsteps fading behind the click of the door. I lie still for a moment longer, my body sinking into the warmth of the table. Everything feels tender. Not sore—just exposed.

I carry Tom's words with me as I walk back to the car. It's time to take care of myself, I realize. I hear it layered with my therapist's voice: *Be easy on yourself. This kind of grief takes time.*

Later that afternoon, I sit alone at the edge of the soccer field, shoes damp from the grass. The air smells of wet dirt and sun-warmed grass. Parents call out encouragement. Ryan runs—small and fast against the open field.

He glances over once. I raise a hand to let him know I'm here.

He turns back to the game, and I hold the moment close.

Chapter 39
The End of Believing

Even in the thick of grief, there were moments that made me laugh. Moments tangled in sadness. This one happened in May.

A month earlier, I'd moved Ryan to a new school—a small Catholic private school just a few miles away. I wanted a place that would hold him not only academically, but emotionally and spiritually too. When he shadowed there, the class had prepared a folded name tent for his desk that said *Welcome Ryan*, each student's name signed around it in bright marker. He came home beaming, already excited. "They have triangle-shaped pizza," he told me. "At my old school, the pizza was square and wrapped in plastic. This one comes off the pan and they put it on a plate." That tiny difference said everything—it felt like care.

The cafeteria there wasn't just a lunchroom. Everything was homemade, prepared with care by parents who took turns helping in the kitchen. It wasn't fancy, just genuine.

By May, he had settled in. The uniforms, the weekly chapel, the sense of closeness that came from everyone knowing each other—it all seemed to ground him.

We hadn't raised the boys Catholic, despite both Tom and

me growing up in the faith. Tom had felt strongly that our kids should be free to explore and choose their own path when it came to religion. But after he died, I found myself reaching back toward the faith I'd mostly set aside. I needed something to hold on to. I needed to believe.

On an ordinary weekday afternoon, Ryan came home from school looking troubled. He dropped his backpack on the floor and blurted, "Some kids at school were talking about Santa."

"Oh yeah?" I said.

"They said he's not real! They said the parents buy the presents and just pretend they're from him."

Now, in prior years, I'd dodged this conversation by asking a question of my own. Once, while driving, Ryan had brought it up: "I heard the parents are the ones who buy the presents."

"Really?" I replied, pretending to be shocked.

"Yeah. But you don't make a lot of money," he said matter-of-factly, "so I know they're wrong."

But this time, he wasn't giving me an out. He stood in front of me, arms crossed, eyes locked onto mine.

"Is Santa real?" he asked.

"What do you think?" I stalled.

"Mom. Come on. Just tell me," he insisted.

"Do you really want to know, Ryan?" I asked.

"Yes," he said.

When I told him the truth, his face fell. He started to cry —real tears, the kind that come from deep disappointment. Ryan had been sleeping in his own bed again for several months but that night, he asked if he could sleep in mine. Of course, I let him.

For a while we lay in silence, the weight of it between us. Then, out of nowhere, he lifted his head.

"What about the Easter Bunny?"

I gave a small shrug.

"Oh. My. GOD," he gasped. "I suppose the Tooth Fairy isn't real either?!"

I couldn't help it—I burst out laughing. The absurdity. The timing. The unraveling of childhood myths, one after the other, in the dark of my bedroom.

Why on earth were the Catholic school kids talking about Santa Claus in May?

When Conor was five, the magic was still alive and pulsing through our house like electricity. This was before Ryan was born, before grief had entered our vocabulary. I was working twelve-hour night shifts in the pediatric ICU then; holidays didn't always line up neatly. That year, Conor had asked for a real bike. Not a tricycle. A big-kid bike. We found a used one, repainted it, and added training wheels. Not because we couldn't afford a new one, but because it didn't make sense to spend a lot on something he'd outgrow in a year.

On Christmas Eve, before heading to the hospital, I gave him a bath. The bathroom window opened up into our screened-in porch. After the gifts had been placed under the tree, Tom slipped outside and shook a little bell.

Ring, ring, ring.

I gasped. "Did you hear that, Conor?" I whispered.

His eyes went wide with wonder. "It's the Chris-i-mus!" he declared. Not Santa. Not Saint Nick. The Chris-i-mus. He shot out of the tub, dripping wet, barely pausing to be dried off. He ran through the house half-dressed, hoping to catch a glimpse—not to see if it was real. There wasn't a doubt in his mind. He just wanted to play with Santa.

Years later, when Conor found out the truth, it wasn't a big deal. He came home, shrugged, and told us how it was— just another kid who'd cracked the code. Then he went outside to play.

But when it came to Ryan, we asked him to play it differently.

"Don't ruin it for your brother," we said.

"Remember how magical it was for you," Tom added. "Don't rob Ryan of that."

Conor took it to heart. That year, he helped Ryan write a letter to Santa—but it wasn't your typical wish list. Ryan asked if Santa was having a good night, offered cookies to help fuel the long journey, and even inquired which reindeer was his favorite.

Then Conor—sweet, secretly-knowing Conor—wrote back as Santa. He printed the letter in careful block letters and placed it near the now-empty plate where the cookies had been, sprinkled with a few leftover crumbs.

A few years later, the Tooth Fairy incident happened—when we'd first moved into our house. Ryan had lost a tooth and tried to wash it in the bathroom sink—only to watch it slip through his fingers and disappear down the drain.

He was distraught. But Tom, ever quick on his feet, said, "It's okay, buddy. The Tooth Fairy is magic. She's kind of like a ghost—she can go down the drainpipe and find it."

"Really?"

"Absolutely. We'll just leave a note under your pillow so she knows what happened."

So we did.

Now, here we were, in May—years later—with Ryan curled beside me in bed, eyes red and puffy, absorbing a different kind of loss.

The illusion was gone. With it, another small piece of his dad.

Chapter 40
Glutes, Grit, and
Other Truths

We start in waves. By the time mine takes off, most runners are already far along. Of the six in our group, only three of us are going the full fourteen. The others peel off earlier. We spread out quickly, each finding our own pace. I fall into mine.

The trail begins on a wide, paved fire road, then slips into single-track—shaded, quiet, and cool. Towering redwoods stretch overhead. Ferns and damp earth line the path. I breathe it in, letting it settle me.

A few miles in, my left knee begins to complain. The hills make it worse. Every incline pulls at something tight, something not quite right. I reach the falls and take a photo as proof: I made it. But I don't linger. I know the hardest part is still ahead. I start to wonder if I'm the last one left out here.

When I spot the aid station still open, I nearly tear up. It's not packed up. There's still Gatorade. More importantly, people. A few teammates appear just ahead, and I don't feel quite so alone.

At the finish, the team is already digging into the potluck. My carpool buddies wait patiently. I'm not hungry—just wrung out. I grab a cup of coffee, a nectarine, a bit of salad. I sip my recovery drink on the drive home, knee throbbing.

Three days later, the knee is still mad. I don't have time to mess around with injuries, so I book an appointment with Kris —my favorite sports massage therapist and a coach with Team in Training (TNT), the Leukemia & Lymphoma Society endurance program I've joined for my next race.

She's fixed me before. She's also told me when to back off. I'm hoping today isn't one of those days.

The session starts mild—testing range of motion, poking here, prodding there. She stretches my legs out straight, eyes narrowed.

"Left side's sitting high," she says. "Not longer—just off."

She rolls me onto my side and starts in on my lateral thigh. I squirm. Grit my teeth. She hands me a stress ball.

"I thought you said you were foam rolling?" she asks, half teasing. "Because I'm barely pressing."

Apparently, I've been doing it wrong. And my glutes? Not pulling their weight.

"They need to join the team," she says.

Translation: I have a lazy ass.

When she's done, I limp to the stretch room, then into an ice bath. I leave with a new list of exercises, foam roller drills, and a glimmer of hope for buns of steel.

That evening, I head to the track. I'm not cleared to run fully—but I'm not cleared to sit on the couch either. I jog slowly, testing it. By the time we start drills—high knees, butt kicks, karaoke—I feel okay.

I join a group running two-lap intervals. I aim for four minutes per interval and hit 3:53. Again. Again. For a moment, I feel strong—until pain creeps in on the fifth repeat, and I back off.

Later, I sit on the couch, trying to isolate one glute at a time without letting my thigh or back take over. It's harder than it sounds. I finish the "glute-ups," reach for an ice pack, and make a sweet discovery: a square of dark chocolate hiding in the freezer.

Of course I eat it.

I carry Kris's advice and the new drills with me. I have more miles in the weeks ahead.

Chapter 41
The Imprint

The downstairs hall closet holds a jumble of things—appliances we don't use every day, stacks of salad bowls, and a shelf crowded with games. Our collection keeps growing, but the ones we no longer reach for—*Candy Land, Twister, Life*—are shoved to the back. That's where the imprint waits—hidden behind the games.

I drag a stool from the kitchen and wrestle the finicky closet door, lifting it with both hands to free it from its track. Climbing up, I reach past the boxes and pull the mold out from behind them. I carry it carefully to the table and set it down.

The clay looks softer than I remember—like dough, but sturdier than it seems. Across the surface, in uneven handwriting, one of the kids scrawled *Thomas – Dad*. I catch myself wanting to wipe it away, then stop. If I'd seen them with the pen, I would have prevented it. Now, I let it be.

I sit, close my eyes, and slide my hand into the shallow imprint, feeling the grooves and ridges of his hand. I try to imagine it coming to life, his fingers interlacing with mine. But there is only stillness—just as there was on his final day, when I held his hand as he took his last breaths.

It happened faster than any of us expected. The social worker had promised to come later in the week to help the boys make the imprint with Tom. But before she could return, he was gone. After the nurse came out to pronounce his death, I told her about the promise, about how much it meant to the boys—especially Ryan. I told her I would not let his body be taken until the imprint was made. She drove to the craft store, bought the clay and a mold, and returned to the house.

The boys were still at school when we pressed Tom's hand into the clay. I set it aside to dry. I kept his body there until they came home, in case they wanted to sit with him—to say goodbye. Later that afternoon, Conor stood in the doorway, quiet, watching but not stepping closer. Ryan went to the bedside with me, his small hand reaching for Tom's as mine had. Then Ryan panicked, crying that we hadn't gotten the imprint. His tears came fast until I showed him what we had made. Relief softened his face as he saw his dad's hand captured there—waiting for him.

We let it dry on the kitchen counter.

Now it waits for all of us—high on the closet shelf, tucked behind the games.

Chapter 42
One Step at a Time

I run solo in the early light, the sky just starting to shift. Each footfall sounds louder in the quiet—rubber on pavement. It's not easy. It never is these days. But I keep going.

I pass a grove of trees, bare branches reaching like questions. I don't have the answers—about who I am now—about where I'm going. I remember a time when I moved easily among people—chatting, connecting, sliding into friendships without effort. These days, even when I show up, I feel like I'm watching from the outside. I forget names. I smile, but it doesn't always reach me.

There's a version of me I can't quite reach—the one who knew herself, who belonged. Sometimes I try to slip back into her shape, but it feels like putting on a jacket that no longer fits.

The void Tom left is still vast. It swallows the moments that should feel joyful. I laugh sometimes, yes—but there's a thin film of numbness over everything. I want to connect. I just don't know how to do it from here.

So I run.

Then one morning, an email arrives from Conor's uncle.

Attached are photos—Conor running cross-country, wind in his hair, sun on his face. Another shows him balanced on a surfboard, his smile easy, his expression calm. He looks healthy. Whole. For the first time in a long while, I let myself believe he might be finding his footing.

A few days later, we get a short call from him. His voice sounds lighter. For a moment, the distance between us feels smaller.

Later, I lace up my shoes again and run.

Chapter 43
Fight Like a Woman

I t's dark outside when I wake. When I step into the hallway, the race hotel hums with quiet energy—women pinning bibs to shirts, sipping coffee, swapping training stories. There's nervous laughter, soft voices, and beneath the tenderness, a deep, unshakable toughness. I eat a banana and a plain bagel. The Clif Bar stays in my pocket—I can't stomach it now. My nerves are louder than my hunger.

I pull on my sweatshirt and board the TNT bus headed for the starting line of the Nike Women's Marathon. It's October 2008.

TNT gives me a place to carry my grief—to move with other people who show up early, run through hard things, and don't always name them.

This is marathon number thirteen for me. For some, that number carries superstition. For me, it feels like defiance. Proof I'm still here.

As the bus rumbles toward the start, my mind drifts back to training.

———

Ryan and I go to the gym pool, trying to cool off during a brutal heat wave. I'm lap swimming when I notice a man standing at the end of my lane.

On my next pass, I stop.

"Do you want to split the lane or circle swim?" I ask.

"Neither," he says, straight-faced.

I hesitate. He adds, "I'm hiding from my son. It's hot, he wants to play rough, and I just want to relax."

I follow his gaze—a boy, already deep in play with Ryan, like they've known each other forever.

I gesture toward them and smile. "Looks like your problem is solved."

I pause my watch and we talk—about the heat, about training. His name is Jeff. He's married.

"Can you believe that my wife did a Team in Training track workout last night?" he says.

"No way," I tell him. "I was there too."

"Her name's Wendy."

"Red hair?" I ask.

"Yes!" he says.

"She's fast!" I say. "I think she won something."

He smiles, proud. "That sounds like her."

I tell him my story—about Tom and why I joined TNT. It's getting easier to say now.

Jeff listens and says, "If you haven't met her yet, we'll have to have you over. She'll love you. And by the looks of it, our boys are going to be good friends."

He's not wrong.

Two days later, I am driving to Wendy's to go for a training run, gripping the steering wheel, nervous about keeping up. It turns out she's not the Wendy I'd remembered.

"Oh, that definitely wasn't me," she says, laughing.

We run and talk like we've known each other a long time. Our paces match. She's sharp and kind, full of the sort of energy that keeps people moving forward. Years later, she'll tell people, *My husband brought me home a girl. He brought me Julie.*

Now, on race morning, Wendy is a few corrals back from me, jumping up and down to stay warm. I stand surrounded by women intent on paces between 6:30 and 9 minutes per mile. We trade nervous chatter and last-minute strategies.

Then a text comes in.

Leave it all on the course.

It's from Coach Jeff.

Six words—and I abandon my conservative plan. I commit from the gun.

Early on, my legs feel heavy. Doubt edges in. I look around at the sea of purple singlets and think about the people we're running for—cancer survivors, honorees, the ones who didn't make it. I think about Tom. I keep moving.

I scan the crowd, hoping to spot Ryan. I don't. The course thins. The noise fades. The aloneness settles in.

Out on the Great Highway, the wind cuts sharp off the water. My legs scream. My pace feels fast, but my watch tells another story. I adjust. I ask more of myself. I stay with it.

I don't ease up.

I leave it on the course.

I cross the finish line wobbling, lightheaded, nearly colliding with the firefighters who hand me a small blue Tiffany box. Inside is a small silver necklace, created just for this race. It feels delicate in my hands—and heavy. Earned.

I'm guided to the medical tent for an IV, foot care, and a cup of warm broth.

Then I hear a familiar voice.

"Mom!"

Ryan's freckled face appears at the edge of the tent, trailed by Jeff, Wendy, and their boys. He throws his arms around me. The hug lands exactly where it's been missing.

———

The following week, Wendy and I meet for a recovery run at a nearby park. A percolation pond runs along one side of the path. On the other, there's a playground and a bocce court. Geese wander the grass, honking and pooping like they own the place.

We fall into an easy rhythm. Our feet move in sync. We don't need words.

Step by step, our friendship takes root.

Chapter 44
Pockets of Light

Gradually, small pockets of space began to open. When Ryan is at practice or playing at a teammate's house, I run. Sometimes short loops, sometimes longer, but they reminded me I was more than a caretaker. After Tom died, I'd lost my bearings—no longer Tom's wife, still a mother, unsure who I was without the roles that had held me. Running grounded me in my body again—reminding me I was still alive.

Meeting Wendy helped too. She folded me into her circle with an ease I hadn't felt in years—dinners, birthdays, laughter.

By then, my closet had gone nearly monochrome. Black. Gray. White. It hadn't been intentional at first. My hand just kept reaching for the same safe pieces. The brighter colors hung to one side, untouched. It was easier not to decide.

One afternoon, Wendy asked gently, "Do you feel like wearing bright colors would be disrespectful to Tom?"

The question startled me. I hadn't framed it that way, but maybe there was something like that underneath. Mostly, I told her, it had just become simpler. Black matched black. I didn't have to think.

"Then let's start small," she said.

We went shopping.

We found a dress with geometric stripes—purple, black, and white. Bold, but anchored in dark. Another for a wedding—blue-green with tiny flowers, a black belt, black trim at the neckline and straps. Color, but edged in something familiar.

For her forty-fifth, we went out to dinner with about a dozen of her closest friends. The night was themed after one of her favorite shows, *Sex and the City*. These women went all out. I wore the striped dress. Heels, too. The night was filled with good food, wine, and laughter that rose and fell like music.

I got used to being one of the ladies.

Months later, we went to dinner at a Cuban restaurant that also had live music and dancing. The room pulsed with rhythm—couples spinning across the floor. I sat watching, content at first, until Wendy came back to the table grinning, urging me to join.

A man appeared beside me, hand extended.

"Come on," he said. "I'll lead."

On the floor, he gave simple instructions. "Look into my eyes," he said. "When I swing you out, always find me again."

The music started. I looked, then looked away, shy.

"I mean it," he said, smiling. "Always find my eyes."

So I did.

And suddenly I was flying—spinning and laughing, squealing like a girl who'd forgotten she knew how. The room blurred. My feet followed his lead. For a few minutes, I wasn't a widow or a mother or anyone's protector. I was just a woman dancing.

When the song ended, he thanked me and said he danced there every week. I never went back. But for one night, I remembered what it felt like to let go—and be pulled back in.

Chapter 45
Letters Home

As summer winds down, football season begins. Ryan wants to follow in his brothers' footsteps—tackle, pads, the whole thing. I try steering him toward flag football, but he and Conor are united. Pop Warner is the only version that counts.

Nervous about the contact, I turn to Tanya, one of the Little League moms whose husband coaches Pop Warner football. She laughs kindly when I admit I'm afraid it will be like the children's movie *The Little Giants*. She assures me it's nothing like it. The players are matched by weight, she explains, and the coaches emphasize technique—how to hit safely, even when it's hard. Her words ease me just enough to let him try.

Through Tanya, I connect with another family—Mark and Lisa—whose son Matthew plays in the same league and goes to Ryan's new school. They offer to help with rides from school to practice, and before long we become friends. Years later, Mark and Lisa will become Ryan's godparents.

The first practices are brutal. The August heat bears down, thick and relentless. They aren't in pads yet—just helmets and T-shirts for the first ten hours of mandatory conditioning. Still, the coaches push them hard: laps, sprints, push-ups.

I sit on the grass with the other parents, the air humming with whistles and shouted commands. Sweat runs down Ryan's neck, his shirt plastered to his back. One of the boys throws up on the side of the field, but practice doesn't stop.

When it's finally over, we drive home with the windows rolled down, breathing in the rush of evening air to counter the smell of sweat-soaked gear—and my son.

I had signed him up half expecting he'd hate it—the strictness, the intensity—and that after one season, he'd be done.

But he loves it. He thrives in it. The structure, the discipline, the physicality give him something he needs but can't yet name. Every tackle, every sprint, every hard hit becomes a release—a way to work through the anger and confusion that's been building inside him since Tom died.

By late fall, the letters begin to settle into a rhythm.

Short notes from Conor—sometimes a paragraph, sometimes just a few lines—arrive every week or two. Usually, there's one for each of us. At the kitchen table, Ryan leans close as I pull out both letters—one for him, one for me. The paper is clean, the edges still crisp. Sometimes he asks about school, the dogs, my running. I can almost hear his voice in the lines, lighter than before.

We don't waste any time writing back. With my help, Ryan writes about school, the dogs, football—how much he misses his brother. I write about Ryan, home, work—whatever surfaces. Mostly, I tell him how proud I am and how much I love him.

By November, one of his letters feels different. It's longer, more thoughtful—written during a retreat with his school. He writes about opening up, about faith and forgiveness, about learning to see his own story in a new light. Between the lines, I can feel him reaching out.

When he comes home for Christmas, the air feels lighter, but a quiet tension sits underneath it. We laugh, share meals, open gifts—but I'm watching, waiting. Without his uncle's steady presence, I'm afraid something might shift. That the progress we've seen won't hold here—with me.

Nothing suggests a step backward, but I can't quite believe it yet.

Chapter 46
Napa Valley:
Miles & Memories

Friday before the race, I'm in my therapist's office. Compassionate and attentive, I've come to think of her as the Good Doctor. I'm curled up on her cozy couch, talking about how the Napa Valley Marathon holds a special place for me—and for Tom.

Napa was our first marathon—the one we circled on the calendar all those years ago after the drive back from Monterey. It's where I set my PR—and where Tom showed up again and again, waiting hours just to see me for a few seconds along the course. I'd be foolish to think running it now wouldn't stir my grief—every place where Tom once waited for me.

So, my therapist and I talk strategy. We decide the best way to handle the grief triggers—those places where I used to see Tom—is to attach a memory to each one. A moment I can look forward to recalling. Like spotting a familiar face on the course—a comfort station for the soul.

Saturday is full. I get Ryan settled at my sister Linda's house, drive to Napa, pick up my bib, eat pasta, and lay out my gear.

Only then do I sit down to finish my memory map—one memory for each place Tom used to stand.

I read for a few minutes before closing my eyes.

Sleep doesn't come.

Instead, I lie awake listening—to every creak, every passing car, the steady drum of rain on the roof. By the time the alarm goes off at 4 a.m., I've barely drifted into anything that resembles rest.

Outside, the rain is cold and steady, but the temperature hovers around fifty degrees—manageable. Joann and Angie both opt for shorts. I pull on capri tights and layer two long-sleeved running tops. I eat a banana and a handful of the M&J's power snacks I brought from home. No coffee. The hotel setup isn't compatible with what I packed and I don't have the energy to care.

We board the bus in the dark.

The ride to Calistoga is quiet. Rain streaks the windows. By the time we arrive at the start, it's clear this isn't a Boston-or-bust day. I let it go.

After changing my mind several times, I ditch the Camel-Bak, my jacket, and even the epi-pen I've carried since child-hood. I'm allergic to honeybees—but today, it's rain, not bees.

Stripped down and committed, I head to the start. The buses pull away.

Joann, Angie, and I plan to line up together. We chat lightly, but I know we won't be running the same race.

A quick stop at the port-a-potty confirms my stomach cramps aren't just nerves. I thank Angie for offering to run with me and tell her it's not my day for a BQ.

I find them again in the corral, and we start together. When the pack begins to move, I wave them on and settle into my own pace.

By mile 6, I reach Lodi Lane and realize it's not the spot I've tied to my first memory. I scan the crowd anyway; the moment drifts past, just out of reach.

A few minutes later, something catches my eye—a bungee cord, lying in the street. Just like the ones from our wedding-day gag. The emotion hits fast and hard, a freight train to the chest. I breathe through it. I can't afford to lose fluids to tears. Pope Street—the real marker—is just ahead.

At mile sixteen, near Oakville Cross Road, I start scanning for baseballs. Of course there aren't any. Still, this was part of the plan—objects, memories, anchors. I high-five a few kids when I hear my name.

"Julie!"

Jen and Jenny—friends of my sister—are waving. I stop for hugs, startled by the joy of being seen.

As I move on, the memory comes: the pitching mound Tom and Conor built in the dirt lot beside our old house. Pitch after pitch. Hours together. Watching *For Love of the Game* before almost every game—Conor imagining himself as Billy Chapel, Tom as his catcher, Gus Sinski. When Conor made varsity, Tom beamed. I did too.

Now the memory lands, sharp. My glute flares, pulling me back into the present. I blink and keep moving.

I try to call up the memory I saved for Tom and Ryan, but I'm not there yet—Yountville Crossing, mile eighteen. Without the marker, it stays foggy. Instead, I think about Tom standing in the cold, race after race, waiting hours just to see me for a few seconds at a time.

The sadness sinks in.

That's when Coach Tim from Team in Training appears. Just like before, he lets me cry on his shoulder—tears, snot, all of it. We jog together a short stretch. When I peel off, I'm steadier.

Ahead, the hill rises.

I hear Tom's voice as clearly as if he's beside me:

Come on, Julie. It's in you. It's in you. Dig deep, baby.

I do.

By mile twenty, I'm still moving.

A medic spots me briefly at an aid station, noticing my limp. I stretch, smile, assure him I'm fine. The road ahead feels endless. I think of Tom taking Ryan to an Easter play—the crucifixion, and the questions afterward about death and what comes next. Tom always said he didn't know for certain—that maybe heaven was real, maybe something else, even reincarnation.

At mile twenty-three, I hear it.

"JULS!"

Dianne—one of the women I trained with for Nike—runs beside me, telling me I look strong. She snaps a picture to prove it.

There are no memories left to reach for now.

I stop looking back. I run.

The final turn comes. I give everything I have left.

I finish in 4:18:10.

I hobble through the chute, watching people embrace, arms draped over sweat-soaked shoulders. There's no one here to greet me. No hug waiting.

My throat tightens. The tears come hard.

Two weeks later, I'm back in the Good Doctor's office. I sit taller this time. Still tired. Still grieving. But steadier.

I tell her about the race—not the time or the hills, but the memories. How I carried Tom with me. How I let pieces of him go, mile by mile.

She listens, then smiles.

"I think this was a turning point for you."

That's when she tells me she's leaving.

I nod.

"I can give you a referral if you want," she says, "but I really think you're okay. You have your grief group. You've done a lot of hard work."

I feel the sadness of another goodbye—but no panic.
I'm still upright.

Chapter 47
Pins and Needles

I woke to the strange sensation of pins and needles running through both feet and ankles, the numbness spreading into my right calf. I hobbled down the hall, blanket around my shoulders, and settled onto the couch, rubbing my legs, willing the feeling back while I watched cartoons on TV.

Later that day I was supposed to go to Great America, the local amusement park, with my best friend, and I was too excited to sleep.

By the end of the first show, the numbness had climbed into my left knee and up my right thigh. I vigorously rubbed my legs and pumped my ankles, rotating them in circles, trying to chase it away. When the next commercial break hit, it had inched farther still. "Conjunction Junction" came on, but I couldn't keep up—my voice lagged behind the words. My mind was elsewhere, caught on the strange, rising void in my legs.

When I tried to stand, my legs wouldn't obey. So I dropped to the floor, forearms pressed into the carpet, army-crawling down the hall with my legs dragging behind me. At the base of the stairs I yelled, "Mom! Jim! There's something wrong with me."

By the time we reached the ER, the numbness had advanced even more. My stepdad Jim stayed beside me while the doctors poked and prodded with Q-tips and safety pins. Then they stepped just outside the curtain, speaking as if I couldn't hear.

"Children from divorced families often rebel when someone new comes into the family. This is likely psychosomatic."

"Are you saying this is all in her head?" Jim asked.

"I'm not crazy!" I shouted, having heard every word.

Jim didn't back down. He insisted on another opinion, refusing to take me home the way the doctor suggested.

Six days in the hospital followed. Tests, scans, more poking. Electrodes were placed along the sides of my head while I watched a computer screen, trying to focus on the flicker of shapes and light.

One test stood out: the myelogram.

I was strapped face down on a tilting table, my cheek pressed against the hard surface, staring at the floor below me. A nurse stood beside me, her voice calm, practiced.

"We're going to clean the area on your back with betadine. It might feel cold."

I couldn't feel it.

"Here comes the needle. It might pinch or feel like pressure."

I didn't feel that either.

They kept asking what I sensed. I searched for it—pain, pressure, anything—but there was only warmth, then light-headedness, then fear.

The table tipped—first slightly, then more. My body shifted with it, strapped in, unable to move. Upside down. Sideways. I stayed fixed in place, watching the floor tilt and slide beneath me.

When it was finally over, they wheeled me upstairs on a

gurney, flat on my back as a precaution. The elevator doors opened and my mom and Jim were waiting just outside the doors. They told me Jim's mom had just had a stroke and was in another hospital. They wanted to see me safely out of the procedure before rushing to her side. I watched as they stepped into the elevator I'd just exited, the doors closing behind them.

Unfortunately, the orderly was long gone—likely assuming my parents or nurse would take me to my room. From the end of the long hallway, I watched doctors and nurses go in and out of rooms. I saw them, but they didn't notice me—even when I waved. So I waited, certain someone would come looking for me.

It wasn't until my best friend and her mom arrived—nearly an hour and a half later—that I was finally pushed back inside. They maneuvered the gurney close to the bed and helped me scoot over carefully, keeping me flat.

The lunch tray arrived just as we got to the room, piled high with everything I'd circled on the menu. My friend fed me—one for you, one for me—until my nurse burst in.

"She's not supposed to be eating anything right now!" she snapped.

My friend's mom leapt up, furious. "Where have you been? We found her left in the hallway—alone—for over an hour!"

The nurse softened immediately, backpedaling. "Since you've eaten, I guess you're not nauseated."

"I'm fine," I said. "The fries were good but the sandwich was kind of dry."

On day five, the doctors explained: my own body had been attacking the coating around my nerves and spinal cord. An autoimmune disease, they called it. Demyelination. The signals couldn't travel—that was why my legs wouldn't work. I was lucky—it hadn't touched my diaphragm. If it had, I'd be on a ventilator. By then, sensation was starting to return.

On day six, I left with crutches, some hope, and no real name for what happened.

Even now, the effects linger. My right foot still catches and drags, especially when I'm tired. Sometimes it's subtle, just enough to scrape my toe against the pavement. On the treadmill, I hear the faint scrape of my toe against the belt when it doesn't quite clear. I pull my knee up higher, dorsiflex harder, willing the foot to follow.

Running magnifies it. On long runs, fatigue makes the weakness more pronounced. On my 40th birthday, I had to get stitches in my left palm after a trip and fall mid-run. No matter how strong I've grown, the weakness never fully disappears.

It's a small thing most of the time, something I adjust for without thinking. But every scrape of that toe, every stumble or fall, carries an echo of that eighth-grade morning when I army-crawled down the hall.

Chapter 48
The Anniversary Effect

I am not ready to meet the day—especially today, the second anniversary of Tom's death. The throbbing in my head brings me back to the first few days after he died. I roll over in bed and pull the covers over my head.

The darkness beneath the covers offers a false respite. The magnitude of being the sole surviving parent feels so large it hurts. I feel helpless doing this alone—but I have no choice in it. My boys are depending on me to figure it out.

This past year has been especially hard. Conor is still gone, and even our few exchanged words can't fill the space he's left. Ryan misses him terribly, and I carry the weight of separating them so soon after losing their dad.

So many people told me that getting past the first year would somehow heal me. Even my mom, who lost my stepdad a year and a half before, said, "Now that the first year is finishing, things will be so much better."

Why did I believe that? I knew better.

"It gets better," the widows and counselors said. "But it's never over."

I hear Ryan in the bathroom. I wipe the tears from my eyes and get up to find caffeine and ibuprofen. Ryan has a baseball game, and I have a long run on my marathon training schedule. I don't want to do either. The gray sky outside isn't helping.

An hour and a half later, I drop Ryan off at the field for pre-game warm-ups. Reluctantly, I drive to the gym for a treadmill run. It's not exactly what my training plan calls for, but my head hurts and all I want is to crawl back in bed. I think about doing just that. Then I hear a familiar voice in my head.

"Come on, Julie. You're tougher than this," Tom says.

I groan.

"Okay. But if there aren't any parking spots, I'm skipping it," I mutter. "I will NOT drive around the parking lot more than once."

He's silent as I pull into a nearly empty lot—a rare event. I walk inside, still bargaining.

I look over at the rows of treadmills. Nearly all of them are free. Even my favorite ones with the wood-like slatted panels. I climb on, start up the running playlist on my phone, and begin at a nice, easy pace. My head throbs. I grip the side rails and close my eyes for a couple of deep breaths. I try to imagine a vacuum-like cord gently removing the pain from my body.

It doesn't help much, and now I'm angry. Angry that I'm in pain. Angry that I've gone through so much and it still isn't enough. Why do I have to feel like shit every year—on holidays, anniversaries, birthdays, and random Tuesdays?

Lately, I've been reliving some of the events leading up to Tom's death in my dreams. I ramp up the speed, letting the anger fuel my stride. My head pounds harder. I turn up the music, hoping distraction will help. It doesn't. I ease back down, grab the rails again, and breathe.

Then *Death Cab for Cutie*'s "I Will Possess Your Heart" comes on. The musical build-up is soothing, at first. But when the lyrics start—five minutes in—I unravel. The thought of giving my heart to someone again, risking sickness, risking death, risking loss… it's too much. I reach to change the song just as a text comes in.

"Thinking of you today. I feel your pain."

WHAT?

No, you don't.

I can't say exactly what happens next. Suddenly, I'm on the ground behind the treadmill, staring up at the ceiling. A small crowd gathers. My leg burns. My head is foggy. Someone stops the treadmill and gently lifts my leg off the belt.

They help me over to the table and chair area. Someone in charge starts firing questions:

"What caused the fall?"

"I tripped."

"Is there someone who can come pick you up?"

"No."

But I have questions too: *Was this a dream? Where's Ryan?* I glance at my phone. It's the 21st. March 21st. Of course it's real.

"Do you have a headache?"

"Yes. But I woke up with it."

She gives me a concerned look.

"Today is the anniversary of my husband's death," I explain. "I woke up feeling bad. My son is at a baseball game. I need to get to the field. I'm fine."

I stand up and walk out.

The baseball game is just getting started when I arrive. Ryan is in the dugout with his teammates. I wave at him, then climb into the bleachers beside the other baseball moms. The hooting and hollering begins. I focus on Ryan—his energy, his smile.

He has already learned to hide sadness too. He brought up

the anniversary several times this week, but today his blue-green eyes sparkle. He wears a sweet smile across his freckled cheeks.

The score, as always, is "fun to fun." Though it looks like the other team's having a bit more fun than we are.

I leave the stands to get a break. I need a few minutes without the brave face. I walk toward the parking lot, aiming for the minivan. Almost there, I run into a mom I haven't seen in a while.

"How are you doing, Julie?" she asks. "I haven't seen you in ages."

"I'm okay," I say with the canned answer I've been giving since Tom died.

She smiles. "Well, it's good to see you." Then she heads toward the field.

I breathe a sigh of relief.

The cheers from the surrounding fields are dulled in the minivan. My head welcomes the quiet. But I notice something —an odd sensation at the crown of my head. I reach up and find a tender, wet spot. When I pull my hand away, there's blood.

Apparently, my treadmill-versus-runner incident was more serious than I thought.

Thankfully, the game ends soon after that. Ryan heads to the neighbor's house to play for a while, and I go inside to clean up my leg and head. Those beloved slats on my no-longer-favorite treadmill really did a number on me. My leg has not one but two wounds: one on the side of my upper thigh, and a second that stretches from the back of my knee all the way to my ankle—spanning the width of my calf muscle. I think about the dirt and germs from everyone's shoes now embedded in my body.

I take a couple Advil and lay down. The day is only half over.

That evening, we have plans to meet up with Tom's and

my old meditation community for a solstice celebration. I think about skipping it—but these people feel easier to be around. They don't ask how I am. They just notice, hold space, and let me exist without needing to explain. I call a couple who live nearby and ask for a ride.

"Would you mind picking us up?" I ask. "I don't think I should drive."

Although Ryan is having fun at the neighbor's, he's happy to come along. These are people who love and miss his dad. He's open with them, even sheds a few tears in the safety of a warm embrace.

The gathering is good for me, too. I don't have to fake a smile here. I can just be with whatever the day brings. There's food, guitar playing, and even some singing. By the time we get home, I'm pretty sure I have a concussion—but I feel okay enough to sleep.

Still, I wake myself several times during the night to do neurologic checks—walking to the bathroom, checking my pupils, making sure no new symptoms have appeared.

It's still dark out, I'm wide awake. My head aches, but it's my leg that screams for attention. I call the advice nurse and arrange to be seen.

Later, Ryan is back at the neighbor's while another neighbor drives me to urgent care. A CT scan confirms the concussion, rules out a brain bleed or skull fracture. I go home with painkillers and antibiotic ointment.

Over the next day, the symptoms worsen. Vertigo. Nausea. Vomiting. Light sensitivity. Images of the fall visit me in my sleep. Most of them are after it happened—the small crowd gathered behind the treadmill, calling my sister Carol through tears, feeling like everyone was staring at me when all I wanted was to hide.

Later, I call the gym to ask if anyone witnessed more than

I remember. I speak to Sue, the woman who helped me that day.

"The fall was witnessed by another member," she says. "They said you didn't tumble. It didn't look like you caught your foot or tripped. You just… fell."

"Did I lose consciousness?" I ask.

"No," she replies. "Everyone said you didn't lose consciousness at any point."

I tell her I've been diagnosed with a concussion. She sounds horrified.

"Oh no," she says. "I asked if you hit your head and you denied it."

"I know," I say. "I remember you even touched my head to check."

That call doesn't bring all the answers, but it helps. Afterward, I dream about the fall again—this time, in more detail. Maybe it's imagined. Maybe it's memory.

I fall forward, landing on the front of the treadmill. Embarrassed, I try to get up quickly. That's when I slam my head into the control panel above me.

Ouch.

I fall back, landing on my right thigh. My other leg catches the belt. The room spins as I'm whipped around and dragged toward the back. On the way down, I clip the left side of my head on the side bar.

After several days, the dizziness subsides. The headache lightens. I don't have to sleep all day anymore—or maybe I just can't. My leg is hot, swollen, red, and so sensitive that even the sheet grazing it is unbearable. I try to sleep on my stomach, but my back aches within an hour.

I pace. I can't get comfortable. When I walk—or even stand—it feels like my leg is on fire. Sitting brings a different kind of pain, the calf muscle shifting under skin stretched beyond its limits.

I call the advice line and get a prescription for antibiotic ointment.

Later that afternoon, I leave for the pharmacy. I wear a cap and sunglasses to shield my eyes from the setting sun. The stop-and-go traffic does its best to make me vomit.

At the pharmacy, I'm hyper-aware of the heads turning. I'm all beat up, with a pained look on my face. I catch the expressions. The gasps.

"Treadmill," I mutter to a few of them, hobbling to the window.

I used to work here as a research nurse, so I'm lucky to catch the attention of Mary, one of the medical assistants. After hearing about my fall, she ducks into the already-closed Minor Injury Clinic to see if I can be seen.

Moments later, I'm ushered in for a good wound cleaning and dressing. She advises me to take the strongest pain med I have before bed. They book me for a follow-up in the morning.

The next day, the doctor examines my leg, doubles my antibiotic dose, and reviews my symptoms. He shakes her head gently.

"You're doing too much," he says.

He writes me a note: one week off work, half days the week after. He stresses the danger of falling again within the first year of a concussion.

"No running for a full month."

Chapter 49
Surrender

By mid-2009, change is constant. The company I joined in September 2007 has just been acquired. In the months that follow, colleagues re-interview for their own jobs; some are let go altogether. Those of us who remain soon learn that our office in Palo Alto is closing, and we'll have to move north to Foster City.

My 40-minute commute more than doubles, stretching to an hour and a half each way on a good day. It feels like one more burden added to the pile.

I lean on church even more during this season. Communion becomes the part I feel I need most. Each week, I find myself waiting for the ring of the bell—noticing how it settles something in me. After I receive communion and return to my pew, I kneel while the rest of the congregation files forward. I thank God for watching over me, then talk to Tom.

I'm not good at surrender. Letting go doesn't come naturally to me—it never has. I can trace that resistance back to the schoolyard.

———

We had been hiding in the bathroom for five minutes, waiting out a gang of boys who threatened to give us cooties. Lunch recess was nearly half over, and I didn't want to waste it in there. But the boys waited just outside the door, pressed behind the cement pillars on either side.

We decided to make a run for it. Catherine bolted right, Cindy left, and I sprinted straight down the middle. The boys split off, each chasing one of us.

Ben found me crouched behind a tree, gripping a jump rope and pointing it at me like a transmitter for the dreaded disease. Instinct took over. In an instant, I grab the rope, twisting it from his hands. Then I tied him to the tree, and ran off to the jungle gym.

Back in class, I noticed Ben's empty chair.

"Where's Ben?" the teacher asked.

"Julie tied him to a tree," the boys sang.

The room erupted in laughter. I was sent to the office, one of the boys dispatched to set Ben free.

"He was going to give me the cooties!" I said in my defense.

The teacher sighed. "Go," pointing towards the door.

I went.

Even then, I couldn't stand still when fear came too close. The instinct to fight back has always been stronger than the instinct to surrender.

Faith asks for something different. Not strength, but trust.

———

Not long after Tom died, my next-door neighbor—Mr. Good Neighbor—asked if he could tend the rose bushes out front. They had begun to thin and droop.

He showed up with his special chicken-poop mix and worked the soil like it was his own.

It felt like more than I could return. I didn't stop him.

After that, I didn't always see him come and go. Sometimes I'd catch the smell of it before I knew he'd been there.

Spring after spring, and even in the fall, he kept at it. The roses bloom outside my window—sometimes full and wild, sometimes thinner—but they bloom.

Chapter 50
Held Together

My wedding anniversary arrives quietly.

I don't mark it in any particular way, but I feel it as the day moves along. By evening, the house settles. Ryan sits at the dining room table, working through his homework, papers spread out in front of him. I stay nearby, moving between the kitchen and the living room in case he needs help.

I head upstairs and pull the quilt from the closet. It rests inside its bag. She made that too—from one of his shirts.

I loosen the drawstring and reach inside, feeling the soft, familiar fabric.

The quilt unfolds easily in my hands.

It's not heavy—wide and square, soft and warm, made to hold one at a time. Each block is made from my favorite shirts of his. Patterns I recognize without thinking. Fabric I've folded, washed, watched him wear.

I carry it downstairs and settle onto the couch with a glass of wine, tucking it around my legs, pulling it up over my shoulders. I lift it briefly to my face, breathing it in.

There are small hearts stitched into the center of each block. I trace one with my finger, following the thread as it loops and curves, the stitching slightly raised beneath my touch. I take a sip of cabernet.

For a while, it's just me.

I listen to Ryan shifting in his chair, the scratch of pencil on paper, the quiet pause as he works through a problem. A few minutes later, he gathers his things and comes over, dropping onto the couch beside me.

I lift the edge of the quilt and pull it across him, adjusting it so it covers both of us.

He leans in, shoulder to shoulder. I hand him the remote. He turns on the TV. The screen casts a soft glow across the room. I watch him as he settles into his show—laughing now and again.

Chapter 51
Santa Barbara

Race morning comes too fast.

I almost didn't make it here.

I'm up at 4 a.m. and out the door an hour later with my dear friend Mark, my son's godfather, who is running his first marathon. We're both buzzing with nerves and caffeine-free adrenaline when our ride pulls up. Out jumps Coach Jeff, dressed in full holiday flair: a Santa hat with attached yarn braids and a Mrs. Claus-style red skirt that falls just below his running shorts.

It's ridiculous. It's perfect. I immediately dub him Ms. Santa Barbara.

Normally, I race alone. I'd only tried having a pacer once before, at the California International Marathon (CIM). My sister Linda jumped in to help mid-race, but I was running on an undiagnosed fracture and wasn't in the headspace for her direct, well-intentioned encouragement. I finished, but it convinced me I did better solo—at least then, when my grief was still raw.

Jeff isn't Linda. He's been coaching me for years and reading my blog for even longer. He knows my quirks, my hang-ups, and how deeply I crave not just a finish, but a race that feels like redemption.

The energy builds as we arrive at the start. Runners huddle in the cool morning air, laughter bubbling up alongside nerves. Mark and I pin our bibs, make last-minute trips to the port-o-potties, and settle into the crowd.

Jeff's braids bounce as he jokes with kids, who giggle and point. Adults cheer at the sight of him. He soaks it in.

This will be a good day.

The course takes us on two loops through Goleta, giving spectators the chance to see us more than once. Jeff waves to the kids, and shows some leg for the adults. Mark settles into his rhythm for his first marathon, while Jeff keeps stride beside me, every step.

The first half of the race is pure fun.

Jeff delivers encouragement with precision—extrapolating my pace when I can't think, telling me I look strong when I feel weak. When the hills rise up, he says, "You eat hills for breakfast."

I allow myself to believe him—even when Ms. Garminia tells me otherwise. I keep pushing.

The course is tougher than expected. With each step, my legs throb from the constant pounding of the pavement and the unrelenting hills. My mind wavers, but I don't give up.

Just before the finish line, Jeff's son runs out to join us. Letting me take the lead, Jeff scoops him up, smiling for the camera as they cross together.

Mark finishes ahead of me, running an impressive 3:57:28 in his first marathon.

I don't hit my BQ—Boston Marathon qualifying time. But I don't give in to defeat either. This race—my fifteenth marathon—is special nonetheless. The course, the company, the absurdity of Ms. Santa Barbara by my side—it all adds up to something I'll never forget.

. . .

That night, Mark, his wife Lisa, and I go out for burgers, fries, and craft beer.

After dinner, we walk to a nearby tattoo parlor in downtown Santa Barbara, where he gets a small tattoo to commemorate the race—a winged running shoe, simple and powerful. Lisa and I stand and watch as it's inked into place.

When he turns to me and asks, "You getting one?"

I smile. "When I qualify for Boston," I say. "That's when I'll get mine."

The Final Stretch

Standing on My Own

Chapter 52
Stronger Still

When I lace up and step into the cold January air, my breath still catches from the tail end of being sick—a rough scrape in my throat with each inhale. The cold air burns for the first few blocks—then it doesn't. My arms loosen. My stride settles. The work grows quieter.

For a long time, I've run waiting for something to give—for pain, for dizziness, for the moment I'd be forced to slow, or stop. But today, I don't. I keep moving.

I think about my wedding ring. Back when I was a new nurse with a steady paycheck, I bought it for myself—a swirl of tiny diamonds I couldn't resist. I wore it on my left hand without much thought, not realizing people would assume Tom and I were engaged. I figured it might keep random guys from hitting on me. Years later, he slid that same ring back onto my finger at our wedding. The circle took on new weight then—commitment, love.

After he died, the ring felt necessary. I wore it like an anchor, a way to keep him close when everything else was unraveling. Eventually, I tried moving it to my right hand, thinking I could reclaim it as my own. But it never quite worked. Too much meaning pressed into the gold band.

Today, just for this run, I take it off.

My finger feels bare, exposed—like I've forgotten my seatbelt. My thumb keeps drifting there, brushing the empty space. I don't know if I'll put it back on.

Tom's ring stays with me. The silver band etched with Celtic spirals hangs from the rearview mirror, catching the light. When the ache swells, I reach for it, closing my hand around the cool metal as if to hold his. Sometimes I whisper hello. Other times, I trace the spirals, remembering the weight of his hand in mine.

A new road opens ahead. A new year, uncharted. Soon I'll start a weekend job at the running store—just four hours a week, a way to stay close to this life, to people who speak in miles and shoes and effort. For now, it's just me and the road. My ponytail swings side to side. Breath and rhythm align. The ground meets me, steady, as I move forward.

Chapter 53
Softening

The yoga studio has just opened nearby. I step inside. Hardwood floors glow under soft light. A fountain trickles in the heated room. It feels welcoming, thoughtfully laid out, as if someone imagined how it might feel to arrive here carrying more than just a body.

I take my first class during the studio's soft opening. I'm intrigued by the invitation to try aerial yoga. Class is held in the larger of the two rooms. Silk hammocks hang from the high ceiling, pooling softly at waist height. The class is playful and unfamiliar. Every pose is supported by fabric. We climb, wrap, lean back, even hang upside down, suspended and laughing as blood rushes to our heads. It feels new. Different. A little daring.

The only part I don't enjoy is savasana. Lying in the hammock, swaying gently from side to side, I grow nauseated. The slow, undulating motion makes my stomach turn. The teacher hands me a ginger candy and helps me onto my mat under the hammock. I suck on the candy and my stomach settles right away.

I sign up for a membership before I leave.

The practice humbles me. I'm stiff and tight, rarely able

to make the shapes the way I think I should. Still, I like asking my body to move differently.

Something about the practice pulls me back.

In my twenties, I took dance classes at the community college —modern, ballet, and jazz. Ballet felt like punishment. The instructor circled the room like a hawk, calling out corrections as she passed.

Pull in your ribs, Julie. Turn out your feet. Lift your chest.

I chased the silence—learning to move in a way that didn't need fixing.

I worked twelve-hour night shifts in the pediatric ICU, but on my breaks I practiced turns in the long breezeway that connected our children's hospital to the adult wing.

One-two-three-turn. One-two-three-turn.

Weeks later, the instructor walked by and said, "Very nice, Julie."

Just that.

I felt lighter hearing it.

Yoga feels different, but the same cues return—pull in your ribs, lift your chest, align your feet. I laugh at myself often at the ridiculous effort it takes to "relax" into a pose, the wobbling, the falling. And I love it.

One night, though, savasana unfolds in a way I don't expect—or want.

With about thirty minutes left in class, restlessness creeps in. My body grows impatient. *When will this end?* Up until then, the practice feels good. We work the spine, loosening and strengthening, drawing energy up and letting it flow. I let myself move freely—stiff or sensual, awkward or fluid. It is enough.

Then the lights dim. The room grows quiet—only breath and the teacher's voice.

We are guided into savasana, corpse pose, and told to imagine preparing for death.

Let go, he says.

Let go of your possessions.

Let go of your home.

Say goodbye to your family.

No, I can't.

The words land too close. I am back in that hospital bed in our family room. Only this time it isn't Tom dying—it's me. My children's faces blur through tears as they hold my hands. I feel myself both as caretaker and as the one dying. The final breath. The body giving way.

My whole body screams *no*.

I cling to breath—because that's what the living do. The meditation moves on, but I refuse to follow. When we are finally asked to picture something that makes us grateful to be alive, I grab hold of the one thought I can.

I am still here.

I carry that thought home with me. When I step through the door, I hug Ryan into my arms and hold him close, whispering how much I love him.

———

The day is already heating up when Cindy and I start running. The hills meet us immediately—not allowing us to warm up before asking us to climb.

The trails are unfamiliar, the turns unclear. At one fork, we guess wrong and find ourselves heading uphill for longer than makes sense. The incline stretches on—longer, steeper—until we stop and look at each other.

This doesn't feel right.

We turn around and circle back, cutting along the edge of what looks like a farm. It's hard to tell. A fence line, dry grass, something just beyond it we can't quite see. We follow the edge until we find our way back to the main trail.

Somewhere along the climb, I notice my shirt clinging to my skin, rubbing against the inside of my upper arms. Without thinking, I lift my arms out to the sides, elbows bent and flared, forearms angled down, creating space between my body and the fabric. The air moves through, cooling my skin.

It feels better.

At the top of the hill, the trail tips downward. I keep my arms lifted as I start the descent, and the air catches more fully now, moving across my chest, under my arms, along my sides.

I widen them without thinking.

The movement shifts. I lean slightly, letting my arms drift from one side to the other, like I'm gliding, the way a child might imagine flying.

For a few strides, I don't think about grief or what I've lost.

Just movement. Just air. Just forward.

I don't care if anyone sees.

Chapter 54
Meeting It Again

By the third anniversary, we think we know what to expect.

We've learned to survive anniversaries by honoring Tom in our own way. We keep these rituals, even after we stop attending grief group.

Ryan is older now, absorbed by school and sports. Two of the families from our small grief group have since moved away.

This year, we plan to honor Tom by riding bikes along the paved trail where we did our long runs. Later, he rode that same path with the boys on their bikes. They'd stop for a slice of pizza along the way, then ride back.

But when I go to wake Ryan, I find him buried under his covers, turned toward the wall.

"I don't want to go," he says, his voice muffled.

The words land hard. It's exactly how I felt on the first two anniversaries—the pull to disappear, to sleep the day away, to let the hours pass without touching them.

We don't ride.

Instead, we spend the day on the couch. The TV murmurs in the background. Time stretches, then blurs. The cushions sag beneath us, warm and unmoving. Neither of us talks much. I watch his chest rise and fall, the way his body curls inward, and I feel the weight of it settle in my own chest.

Later, I remember something the support group facilitator once told us—that kids reprocess grief as they grow, that loss meets them again as they step into new versions of themselves.

At the time, I don't think I understood what she meant.

Now I do.

Chapter 55
Running on Faith

Cold rain pours from the sky in Portland.

I coat my feet in un-petroleum jelly before sliding my toes into the individual pockets of my thin Vibram FiveFingers.

I stare at the slick soles. My pulse quickens.

The walk to the start is short, but my feet are already drenched. My Garmin screen is frozen when I arrive in the start corral.

I jab at the buttons. Nothing.

Coach Jeff calls me with a final pep talk. He's seen the weather report.

"It's just water. You won't melt," he says with a chuckle.

Then, more gently: "Go by feel. You've got this."

The gun goes off, and I find the 3:50 pace team and tuck in behind them. They're doing a run-walk strategy—surges, then walk breaks. I hold steady instead, allowing them to fall back during their walk breaks and get ahead during their run bursts. It works, until someone's keys start jingling with every step.

I move ahead, keeping the group in sight but running my own race.

My Vibrams have smooth soles, not made for slick pavement, and I've never worn them in a downpour. The steady rhythm keeps me warm even though my gloves are soaked.

A few miles in, the rain eases. I see the road now. I trust my footing. Then briefly, the sun breaks through, golden against the wet pavement.

At halfway, I spot friends from my running blog community—right where they promised. I toss them my gloves and jacket and keep moving.

Three-quarters in, I spot a race clock. I do the math, subtracting the lag from start to gun—three minutes? Five? Too close to know. No margin. No room to let up.

The pain hits next. A burn flares at the back of my left heel. Something sharp blooms under the arch of my right foot. I don't look down. I already know.

This is the moment.

I've been running on feel all day—breath, instinct. Faith, made physical. I pick it up. Sub-8:30. Sub-8:15. Sub-8. I pass runner after runner, closing the gap one body at a time.

Two miles out, my body begs me to slow. The noise blurs —music, cheers, signs. I turn inward. This isn't about avoiding failure anymore. It's about claiming what I've earned.

The finish clock reads 4:02:xx as I cross. If I started three to five minutes late, I've done it.

I've finally done it. I've qualified.

I just need proof.

Back at the hotel, I don't even shower.

I go straight to the results page.

Something's wrong.

My race tag failed at key checkpoints—including the finish.

I peel off my Vibrams. The evidence is there: my race tag

shredded, the back of the left foot stained bright red, the front of the right dark with blood. I gave everything.

There isn't the clean record I need. No GPS data. Only the race clock in my finish-line photo and the recorded start delay.

I email Portland race officials. The Boston Athletic Association. Anyone who might help me prove what I know in my bones.

Later, I file the result correction form and pray it's enough —to validate my long-sought BQ and secure the place I've been chasing for nine years—Boston.

Chapter 56
Marked

I cover pages with doodles—spirals, butterflies, geckos. Nothing feels right—too busy, too embellished.

I search for Celtic spirals and find the triskelion—three spirals joined at the center, appearing to move forward without end. I try to fold it into something more: the wings of a butterfly, the body of a gecko. But it's too much. Then, picturing wings or a tail peeking out from my swimsuit, I abandon the idea.

I want a tattoo that means something. Not decoration or for show. Just for me. So I decide on the triskelion alone. Its threefold nature carries its own weight: past, present, future; mind, body, spirit; birth, death, rebirth.

It's simple. Strong enough to stand alone.

At the end of last year in Santa Barbara, Mark had asked if I'd get a tattoo too. I told him, *"When I qualify for Boston."* Now I have.

I drive to a shop to see an artist a friend recommended. It isn't fancy—not the clean, quiet studio I'd pictured. More like a dive bar with fluorescent lights. The space is wide open, with tables set up just far enough apart for artists to circle around. No privacy screens. The place feels sketchy. For a second, I think about leaving. But I don't.

My heart races as I slide my jeans down just enough to expose my hip bone. I turn my head, avoiding eye contact with anyone else in the room. I'm uncomfortable—still sore from Portland, aching all over, and modest in ways this space doesn't allow. The artist notices and drapes a towel across the other side of me.

The machine buzzes, the needle scrapes, and before I can tense, it's done. Quick. Final.

The triskelion now lives on my right hip bone, no larger than a quarter—small, hidden—even in a swimsuit. No one will ever see it unless I choose to show them.

It isn't for anyone else.

It's for me.

The spirals turn. I keep going.

Chapter 57
Submit. Reload. Repeat

Registration for the Boston Marathon opens at 6 a.m. sharp, Pacific time. I'd heard it could sell out before most runners on the West Coast woke up. So I go to bed early, set my alarm for 5:30 a.m., and now I sit in the warmth of my bed, coffee in one hand, laptop balanced on my knees.

The moment the form appears, I pounce. I fly through the basics—name, date of birth, sex, address—then jump straight to the qualifying race: race name, location, finish time. Fingers flying, I hit submit.

Nothing. The page reloads. All the fields blank again. No confirmation. No error.

I tap again. Again. Again.

Each click feels louder. My pulse races. My breath shortens.

Minutes crawl. Half an hour drags by. Then over an hour. My stomach knots. My fingers are damp with pressure.

Finally, the page loads. A blue bar at the top, words I've been straining to see: *Your Boston Marathon application has been received.*

I sink back into the pillows, exhaling in one long rush.

Relief—though not complete. Boston still has to review my application, confirm my Portland time, decide if I'm truly in.

For now, I wait.

———

Weeks later, an email from the Boston Athletic Association appears in my inbox.

I open it, heart thudding, scanning past the formal language until the sentence appears:

Your entry into the 2011 Boston Marathon has been accepted.

For a long moment I just stare at the screen.

After nine years of chasing it, I'm in.

I breathe.

Later that evening, I pour a glass of wine. Ryan celebrates with me in his own way. For the first time, Boston feels real.

Chapter 58
Holidays

It's Thanksgiving, and for the first time in years we spend it with Tom's family. We head to the retreat house in Seal Beach, where fourteen tiny bedrooms line the halls —each with a twin bed, a sink, a flashlight, and a crucifix on the wall. The extended Fergus clan feels right at home here.

Conor has been home since June, back from Hawaii, and he'll stay with us until he leaves for the Air Force in January. For this trip, he flies down two days ahead from home to spend extra time with Dylan while Ryan and I make the long drive south—eight hours of holiday traffic crawling down the 5.

My back aches from sitting, my bladder nags, as we come to the most striking stretch of the drive.

"Ew!" Ryan calls, wrinkling his nose. "What's that smell?"

The smell hits before the view.

I point down toward the muddy pens.

A massive expanse of cattle packed tight behind wire fences. Hides caked with mud. Heads drooping.

"Those cows don't seem happy," he says.

We laugh, plugging our noses.

He decodes the snarky messages from the GPS we've

named Zoey, short for a part of her license plate, ZOJ0—though we always read it as ZOJO.

We talk about how different the roads are here. In Northern California, you have to exit one freeway to get on another. In Southern California, you just slip into the right lane and—voilà—you're swept onto a new freeway without even realizing it.

"Stay awake," I tell him. "Don't let me miss the lane."

He nods, serious now in his role as my co-pilot.

When we finally pull up, the familiar chaos spills out before we even get inside—teasing voices, bursts of laughter, the smell of bacon drifting from the kitchen.

Inside, Conor is already woven back into the family fold, laughing, teasing, arms thrown casually around his brother's shoulders. At the long dining table, someone is setting up a game board. Family gatherings mean games. Scrabble. Charades. Football on the beach. Trivial Pursuit.

The clack of Scrabble tiles folds into laughter and the crash of waves just outside.

I drift back to another Thanksgiving here. Tom once declared the bathroom near the front entry the official Trivial Pursuit Study Area, making fun of his youngest brother, Joe, who used to keep the cards in his own bathroom at home. He taped a sign on the door: *Trivial Pursuit Study Area. Shush. Don't flush.*

Hours later, his older brother walked in carrying a brand-new, still-wrapped edition of the game.

"Study all you want, Joe," he said. "We're playing with this version."

The house erupted.

Another year, Tom gathered everyone for a different game: "Count the Crucifixes." The kids tore from room to room, shouting numbers as they went.

"Fourteen!" someone yelled.

Later, someone unearthed a box in the basement and the total jumped to twenty-seven.

The crucifixes are still there, lining the walls, watching over us as we gather again.

———

Christmas feels harder this year. He's only just come home, and already he's leaving again.

Shopping for Ryan and Dylan is easy. But what do you buy for a son who's leaving for Basic Training in two weeks? He won't be able to take much with him to Basic. I think about emailing his Sergeant for ideas—though I don't even know where he'll be—and picture the fallout: push-ups assigned to the kid whose mom reached out. I close my laptop. Better to miss than embarrass him.

Before returning home from Hawaii, Conor wrote on a blog he'd started about a friendship he'd formed with an older veteran at work—kindness, choosing to show up for someone who had no one else. He also wrote about his uncle, grateful for the steady guidance.

"I guess I'm a lot like my dad," he wrote, "and I don't mind it."

We keep our ornament tradition. Every year, I add one new ornament to the boys' collections—something to capture the year in a single object.

Ryan's is the Eiffel Tower, a nod to his trip to France with his aunt and uncle as part of a larger group of families traveling together. Dylan's is a golf putter, since he spends his weekends on the green. Conor's is a globe—his whole world about to change. Mine is a cloth Christmas tree with sequins, nearly identical to one I was given as a little girl.

At night the tree glows—white lights sparkling against pine branches. The house smells of cookies baking, Christmas music drifting softly through the room.

Conor stretches across the couch, long legs reaching to the far armrest, his feet resting on Ryan's lap. Ryan doesn't protest; he just shifts to make room. Ronin snores at my feet. Laughter bubbles from the boys.

I sit on the love seat and watch.

Chapter 59
March Forth

The thunder of boots rises before I see them—nine hundred airmen striking the pavement in perfect rhythm, the sound swelling until it vibrates in my ribs. Then they appear, a tide of uniforms marching into view, each body hidden behind the same cadence, the same squared shoulders, the same low-brimmed hat. Commands crack through the air, precise and disciplined. Around me, families stretch upward, desperate to separate one face from the sea of sameness, desperate to claim their own.

I scan the rows, my heart racing. In that tide of uniforms, I know one belongs to Conor.

A different image surfaces: the front lawn, years ago, when we first moved into the neighborhood. Conor in a 49ers jersey, Ryan trailing him, the neighbor boys tumbling over each other in the grass. They made friends instantly, the teams dividing the same way each time—Conor and Connor together, Brendan and Ryan on the other side. Ryan wished that he could be on Conor's team, but the lineup never changed. Laughter carried across the yard with the thud of sneakers on grass, jerseys slick with sweat, the smell of freshly cut lawns drifting in the late afternoon sun.

The memory fades.

I squint against the glare, wishing I'd brought my sunglasses. Brass belt buckles flash in the light, the Texas wind pushing grit into my eyes. Dylan nudges me and points.

"Second row. Look toward the end on the right."

I follow his line of sight and finally—there he is.

The commander's voice cuts through the stillness, crisp and sharp, followed by the cadence of the Airman's Creed. Nine hundred voices rise as one, steady and strong, carrying the weight of commitment and pride. The sound vibrates in my chest. Heat shimmers on blacktop, dust lifts into the air, and even from the stands I catch the faint scent of sweat from so many bodies moving as one.

I think of the kitchen table not long before this trip, a job description spread out in front of me. My eyes blur as I read, tears slipping down before I can stop them. Conor looks up, puzzled.

"Mom, why are you crying?"

"It sounds like your job is the bomb-loader tester guy," I say, the words catching in my throat.

He laughs lightly, shaking his head.

"It's not like that. I won't be on the front lines. And it's not like the old movies you see, where people march up to each other with rifles and shoot."

His tone is steady, practiced, as if he's already thought through how to reassure me.

I want to believe him. I want to hold onto his confidence like it could shield him. Even then, all I can think is how heavy the responsibility must feel—carrying weapons built for destruction in his own hands.

Back on the parade grounds, the air shimmers, voices still carrying the creed. I shift my weight, trying to fix the moment in memory, knowing how quickly it will all pass.

I think of the weeks leading up to this day, how I carried my phone everywhere—even into the bathroom—afraid I might miss his call. Conor was allowed to phone home only now and then, privileges earned by good behavior. Each ring sent a jolt through me, the buzz in my hand setting my heart racing. Ryan would drop just about anything, pressing close, his face shining just to hear his brother's scratchy voice through the static. He didn't skip school or practice, but the first thing he asked when I picked him up was always, "Did Conor call?"

The letters came too, folded pages in his familiar scrawl, sometimes short, sometimes thoughtful. Ink smudges left traces of his hand on the page. I asked him to write whenever he could, to let us know he was okay. Every time, I signed off the same way: *I'm so proud of you, Conor. I love you.*

The sound of voices fades, the creed ending, and the formation begins to break. Families surge forward, eyes scanning, hands lifting to point and wave. My pulse quickens, caught between ceremony and reunion.

There he is—breaking from the rows, walking toward us.

Ryan reaches him first, throwing his arms around his brother's waist. Conor bends low, boots squeaking against pavement as he lifts him into a full embrace, Ryan's muffled laugh pressed into his shoulder. When he sets him back down, Ryan grins, cheeks flushed.

Dylan steps in next, steady and composed, pulling Conor into a firm, wordless hug—the kind of embrace that says more than it shows.

Finally, it's my turn. When he steps toward me, I fold into him, arms wrapped tight, unwilling to let go. His shoulders are broader, his back solid under my hands. My boy is now a man.

When we pull apart, Conor leads us across the base,

pointing things out with casual pride. We stop at a row of planes where he gestures toward one.

"This is the A-10," he says, his voice carrying both certainty and excitement.

Ryan leans close, eyes wide, while I take in the vastness of the machine that is now part of his daily life.

We trail after him to the barracks—narrow rows of bunks and lockers, the scent of disinfectant sharp in the air, boots clanging on tile. He shows us where he sleeps, where his things are kept. As he proudly opens his locker, my eyes widen as only a drill sergeant—or a mother—would when I see everything perfectly folded and lined up.

Outside, we pose for a family photo—me in the middle, my arms looped around both Dylan and Conor, Ryan pressed close in front. We are together again—if only for the rest of the day.

Next, we head out for lunch. We walk along the River Walk, a winding stretch of paths lined with shops and restaurants hugging the San Antonio River. Shade cools the path beneath stone bridges, then opens suddenly to sun where café umbrellas bloom. The smell of grilled onions and fresh tortillas drifts across the water. We linger over burgers and fries, grease warm on our fingers, stretching the moment into the limited time we have. Conversation moves between light jokes and heavier pauses, each of us pretending we don't notice how quickly time is moving.

Too soon, our time is up. We drive him back to the base and say our goodbyes. Ryan first—his arms tight around his brother's middle. Dylan next, his hand clapping Conor's back before pulling him close.

Then it's my turn.

I wrap my arms around him and hold on longer than I should—memorizing the heat of his back, the weight of him in my arms.

I finally let go.

Chapter 60
Layers of Hope

The smell of garlic intoxicates me as I stir the meat sauce simmering on the stove. Steam rises, fogging my glasses, the sauce bubbling and popping in the pot. Tom never measured exactly. The lasagna and clam dip recipes I've kept alive since his death survive only in memory —how they tasted when he made them. I scoop a spoonful from the pot, close my eyes, and smile as the flavor hits. It's just how I remember.

It's hard to believe four years have passed since the day I watched a single tear roll down Tom's cheek as his last breath slipped away. Each anniversary lands differently. Today, I'm not worrying about my son overdosing on drugs. I haven't fallen on the treadmill. Ryan isn't buried under his covers refusing to face the day. The day isn't over yet, but it might just be an okay day.

The sadness is still here, but it comes with a thread of acceptance—not relief, exactly, but a sense that we know this terrain now, even as it keeps changing beneath our feet. It doesn't feel quite as heavy—softer around the edges now. The bad days still come—just less often.

We set the steaming pan of lasagna on the table, the smell of tomatoes and cheese spilling into the room, and pause for grace. I keep my prayer simple: gratitude for my boys, for our health, and for the small pieces of happiness we've managed to gather amid the sad moments.

Ryan's prayer is more straightforward: "Thank you for Conor and Dylan. Thank you for my friends. And thank you for Mom and Dad's lasagna. Please tell him we miss him and love him."

"Amen."

I don't yet know how many times grief will circle back for him, how it will meet him again as he grows into new versions of himself. Tonight, I just know we're here—fed, breathing, remembering.

Our glasses—his milk, my cabernet—clink together. Forks scrape plates, the rest of the room quiet. I take a bite, close my eyes, and savor the flavor. For a second, I see Tom across the table, blue eyes glinting, mouth neutral as usual but with a hint of a smile behind his eyes.

"Is it as good as mine?" he teases.

"Close," I answer in my head. "But it'll never be exactly as you made it."

I open my eyes to Ryan watching me. "Do you remember the fart story?" he asks.

I laugh. "How could I forget?"

Dinner with Tom and the boys was never quiet. One night, just as we sat down, one of the boys let one rip. Tom froze mid-motion, raised his fist, and brought it down on the table with mock-serious drama.

"There will be NO. More. Farting. At the table."

The boys paused—until Tom let one go himself. The room exploded with laughter. Both boys nearly fell out of their chairs.

Ryan and I laugh out loud remembering it now.

"When Conor comes home on leave, are you going to make lasagna again?" Ryan asks.

"Maybe," I say. "Or maybe one of Dad's steak dinners—Conor always loved those more."

Ryan nods, satisfied. Already we're imagining the meal, the laughter, the table full again.

The Finish Line
A New Kind of Peace

Chapter 61
Boston Bound

The suitcase sits open on the floor, half-swallowed by a week's worth of tossing things in. Running shoes rest beside one corner, a ziplock bag of gels, folded shirts, tights, socks, and a running hat—everything I might need for whatever weather Boston decides to deliver. With one day left before I fly to Boston, I go through my packing list carefully. The paper crinkles in my hands as I check each item—then check again. It's the same list I've used for every marathon— familiar, reliable. I've expanded it for this trip.

Beside my bag, Ryan's half-zipped suitcase waits. He tugs it shut, only to open it again and add one more thing. His excitement fills the room—a low hum of energy that matches my own.

It took me nine years to get here. Some of those miles were with Tom, many without him. Now the steps feel different—not desperate, but deliberate. I stand on the edge of Boston.

This isn't just any race. It's the 115th Boston Marathon.

Boston holds all of it—the years of training, injuries, near- misses, and the grief that reshaped my life along the way. Standing on that start line will mean more than miles. It will mean I've survived—and that my boys have too. For the first time in years, I believe I've earned my place there.

But Boston isn't the end.

Thirteen days later, I will line up again—this time on the rugged coast of California—for the Big Sur Marathon. Together, the two races form the Boston to Big Sur Challenge. A little crazy, but it may be my only chance. The Boston Athletic Association is already tightening qualification times and changing the registration process. If I want to do this, now is the time.

Big Sur has always been one of our favorites—the most beautiful marathon I know. I picture Hurricane Point, where Taiko Drummers drive their rhythms into tired legs, urging us up the climb. At the crest, a grand piano floats through the air as runners cross the Bixby Bridge—ocean on one side, rolling green hills on the other.

This year, though, I won't get to see the happy cows grazing along the course. A landslide on Highway 1 has turned it into an out-and-back. Different, but still Big Sur.

I'm still thinking about all of it when an email lands in my inbox.

It's from Vince, one of my blog readers—a "Short Boston Primer." He paints the whole weekend: Celtics playoffs, Red Sox at home, Patriots' Day ceremonies across the city. Sunday morning, runners stream through neighborhoods on easy shakeout runs—nodding, waving, a quiet club of thousands from around the world. It's like the "Pro Bowl," he writes—a collective reward.

Then his best part: after the bus drops you in Hopkinton, walking that quarter mile to Athlete's Village—tell yourself there is absolutely no place you would rather be in the world at this very moment. The happiest place in the world, and as close as you'll get to being an Olympic athlete. Meet and greet the runners and hear their stories. Of course the pain is yet to come.

I wipe away a few happy tears, thank Vince for his email, and return to the piles on the floor. The rustle of clothes, the scrape of zippers, the careful placement of shoes against the hardwood—each sound reminds me I'm really going. Soon the suitcases will be zipped, but not yet. I'm still circling the last-minute items, still triple-checking the list.

Ryan appears in the doorway clutching Beary, the stuffed bear that once propped up my belly while he grew inside me. Now, twelve years later, Beary is still here—tucked under Ryan's arm, his fur worn soft from years of love, a red heart-shaped patch stitched across his chest from when Ronin tore him open as a puppy. We turned it into a full surgical procedure— stuffing returned, careful stitches, the patch sealing him up. He sets the bear on top of his clothes, certain it will make the trip.

Chapter 62
Boston

Runners pour in from around the world, and Boston vibrates with anticipation.

On Saturday, Ryan and I head to the race expo. The place is electric—booths bursting with gear, runners weaving through aisles with nervous smiles. The moment I spot the Boston Marathon jackets, I make a beeline for them. I've been dreaming of this jacket for years. When Ryan asks if I'll get him one too, I tell him it's something you have to earn. He smiles and says he will someday.

At the poster-making station, Ryan creates a bright green *Go Mom* sign in bold strokes. I make one too: *Run Wickedly Awesome!*—a nod to the city and to the runners I'll soon join. We walk a few blocks to Boylston and snap a photo at the finish line painted on the pavement.

I've stood here once before—with Tom and the boys on a trip years ago. We were on our way to the Berkshires to see Dylan in a play. He called it a detour, "inspiration for your BQ," but I knew he brought us for more than the race. He wanted to plant the dream in all of us.

The weekend continues with brunch at Kurt's house, a

long-time blog reader who invited Ryan and me to join him and his girlfriend while we were in town. His living room hums with voices—runners of every speed, from first-timers to those who will toe the line near the elites. Ryan fits easily among them, soaking in stories as if they're old friends. Kurt's warmth steadies me. I feel at ease here.

Monday. Patriot's Day.

A state holiday, but here it's more—a city-wide heartbeat, pulsing through the streets.

At the Athlete's Village, buses roll in and runners spill out. I arrive about forty minutes before my wave is set to start. The cold sinks deep into my fingers despite my gloves. The air hums with anticipation, the kind of stillness that makes you hold your breath. Thousands of runners stretch, jog in place, sip water, or stare silently at the ground. I sit cross-legged on a patch of damp grass, trying not to shiver, trying to stay calm. My thoughts drift—to the years it took to get here, to the miles ahead.

Eventually, we're called by pace to file into the starting corrals. The marathon runs in two waves, each lined up by expected finish time. I shuffle forward with the crowd and remind myself: this is it. My one Boston. My moment to savor.

My fingers and face go numb as I inch forward with more than twenty thousand other runners. The cold doesn't matter as much as the nerves. I don't mind the sardine closeness, huddled together for warmth. My stomach churns. I wonder if the long downhill will shred my legs. I steady my breath.

However much I question my preparation, I remind myself: I earned this. Still, the old doubts whisper—am I good enough, strong enough? For most of my life, those questions weighed on me. But here, standing at this start line, I feel something shift. I am here. That means something.

BANG.

Ready or not, I go.

The sun is bright, the air sharp, the energy electric. I hold back tears crossing the start, struck by how long the road has been. I'm carried forward by a tide of runners. Spectators line the course like a living riverbank—cheering, waving, offering orange slices, Vaseline, and every kind of encouragement. Hand-painted signs bob above the crowd, and bright chalk scrawls stretch across the pavement: *You've got this, Almost there.* Then, just beyond the first water stop, I catch sight of one that makes me laugh out loud—*Go Mom*—the same words Ryan drew yesterday, though not in his handwriting.

I run open, taking it all in. Tom is here too, in the rhythm of my breath, in the beat of my shoes.

In the early miles, the road turns slick with discarded water cups, crunching like confetti underfoot. My feet ache, hips burn, neck tightens from holding my head steady. Sweat gathers in the crease of my elbows, dries sticky on my skin. My breath grows heavier, but I keep going.

By the halfway point, the sun warms my shoulders and I hear the Wellesley scream tunnel before I see it. When I reach the college, students line both sides of the road, packed shoulder to shoulder. It hits like a wall of sound—high-pitched, wild, joyful. I high-five until my hand stings and my arm aches. I can't leave without a kiss.

A mother stands with her daughter off to the side. I point to a sign that reads, *Kiss a Girl,* and ask if I can kiss her cheek. She smiles, nods, even snaps a photo. We all laugh.

Later, near Boston College, I kiss a guy holding a sign that invites it. His friend howls when I go for the cheek instead of his lips, and we all share the joke. The joy is infectious.

Then the course tilts upward. The Newton Hills rise, one after another. Each step lands heavy. My quads scream, calves knot, pace slows—but I don't stop. I dig in. Chalk letters stretch across the pavement: *You are stronger than this hill.* I press harder, holding on to it just long enough to crest the rise.

At last, the final hill falls behind. The CITGO sign appears in the distance. My throat tightens. I dig deeper.

Just before the turn, Dylan's old recording plays through my headphones—layering beats, shakers, and the voices of Tom and the boys from another time:

Tom: "Come on, Julie, it's in you. Dig deep, baby."

Dylan: "Run."

Tom: "Come on, Julie. You're almost there."

Conor: "You can do it. Go Mom. You can do it."

Ryan, sleepily: "Go Mom. You're almost there. You can do it."

I carry their voices as I push forward.

I pass the sign, expecting the finish to come fast. It doesn't.

The road stretches longer, the turn to Boylston still out of reach. My emotions crest. My heart is full and empty at once —grieving all I've lost, grateful for all I've held onto. It's only a race, but it's never been just a race.

Finally, I turn onto Boylston. The street roars. Spectators crowd both sides, their cheers crashing over me. Cowbells clang from the sidewalks, sharp and insistent, layering over the thunder of voices.

My eyes blur. I scan the faces, desperate to find Ryan. He's not where Kurt said they'd be. Panic flickers. I don't want to miss him.

Then I see him.

Up ahead, Kurt waves an arm high. Ryan stands beside him, pressed against the railing, waiting. I run over and hug him. His little arms wrap around me with a depth of knowing —he remembers everything we've endured. His hug is comfort, pride, and love all at once.

I pull myself together, wipe my eyes, and push forward.

And when I cross that finish line—the one I've dreamed of for nearly a decade—it feels different than any other. These tears aren't from pain or defeat. They're not from exhaustion. They're tears of becoming.

Impossible may be nothing, but the grit, the blisters, the grief, the persistence—that's something. And this finish line? It means more than all the others.

Because it isn't just where I finish—it's where I begin again.

Epilogue
Here and Now

Just days after Boston, I ran the Big Sur Marathon as part of the Boston-to-Big Sur Challenge—two iconic courses, thirteen days apart. It demanded grit and stubbornness—and I carried it through. Not a quiet fade-out, but a final surge that closed my marathon years with gratitude.

Running is still with me, though it looks different now. My pace is slower, my distances shorter. Yet when I lace up, a breeze moves across my arms and face, the trail crunches beneath my shoes—steady, familiar.

Occasionally I cry. But nothing hurts the way it once did. My grief has settled like the scar on my leg—visible, tender when the weather shifts, but part of me now. I run with that scar. With those memories.

I no longer chase times or personal bests. Running still steadies me, and if my heart calls me there—and my body is willing—I'll line up for another marathon. At times, I catch Tom beside me—in a song, a quiet memory, or in a voice that surfaces when I need it most. I think of the woman I was, lacing up in those early years after he died. I think of the boys, so small and vulnerable then. I think of Tom's voice, still tucked somewhere inside me: *You've got this, Juls. Just keep going.*

I did. I kept going. I kept pace.

Conor runs his own business with a friend, building virtual restaurants—nimble, creative, and determined. When the rules change, he pivots, adjusting his stride without losing sight of the finish line.

Dylan, the boy who was five when I met Tom, is a father himself—reading endlessly to his son, much the way Tom once read to him. I see Tom's tenderness alive in the way Dylan fathers.

Ryan has started talking about running a marathon himself—maybe Napa. The thought of him on that course makes me smile. It even tempts me to lace up again, not to prove anything, but to see if I still can. Or I may choose the sidelines, cheering Ryan on—the way Tom once did for me.

Whether I run another marathon or not, I know what matters most: showing up, one step at a time.

The road that once carried my sorrow now holds my strength. I move through it steady and whole in ways I once thought impossible. Each step forward feels like grace—a quiet reminder that I'm still here, still keeping pace.

And still, some days—like today—the weight of him is everywhere. I carry that too.

Acknowledgments

There are people who stepped in when I couldn't hold everything on my own.

I am deeply grateful to Tom's older brother and his wife for taking Conor into their home during one of the hardest seasons of our lives. They gave him structure, support, and a place to land when I couldn't give him what he needed. Their generosity extended beyond that time in ways that mattered more than I can fully express here.

To my family, who showed up again and again—with meals, with presence, with patience.

To the friends who ran beside me, sat with me, and listened—especially in the days when I didn't know how to keep going.

To the teachers, coaches, and mentors who supported my boys in ways I couldn't always see but deeply felt—thank you for helping guide them forward.

And to my sons—everything begins and ends with you.

Author's Note

In the midst of loss, I began writing in personal journals and on a blog to make sense of my suddenly changed life as a widow and mother of grieving children. Those raw, unfiltered words became my lifeline. I have drawn on them in writing this book, shaping them to fit the voice of this memoir. Memory is imperfect, but I have tried to tell this story as honestly and faithfully as I could.

I did not walk this road alone. Family, friends, neighbors, teachers, coaches, and even strangers helped me and my sons find our footing. Many stepped in at different times—offering guidance, mentorship, encouragement, or simply showing up when we needed it most. Some I knew well; others were part of my sons' lives beyond my direct view. Each, in their own way, helped us keep moving.

This book was also shaped by the act of writing itself. To my blog readers, who held my words in the rawest days of grief; to my teachers and fellow students in Gotham Writers' memoir classes, who pushed me to keep going; and to those who read and offered feedback on early drafts—your insight and encouragement carried me forward.

Finally, to those who may be grieving as they read, I offer

this: you are not behind, you are not broken, and you are not alone. Every step—no matter how unsteady—matters.

I wrote this because I once searched for a story that told the truth about grief—the messy middle, the parenting, the love, the breaking and rebuilding—and couldn't find it. If you are reading this while grieving, I hope these pages have offered companionship on your own road forward.

About the Author

Julie Fergus is a writer, runner, and mother of three. After the death of her husband, Tom, she began writing in journals and on a long-running personal blog as a way to cope with the daily work of grief while raising children who were grieving too. Those early, unfiltered words became the foundation for this memoir, and a community of readers, including some navigating grief themselves, offered encouragement along the way.

Julie has completed more than a dozen marathons, including the Boston Marathon, and running has long been both her refuge and her language for endurance, loss, and forward motion. She is also a yoga teacher and longtime healthcare professional, bringing a grounded, embodied perspective to this story of resilience and healing.

She lives in California, where she continues to run, write, teach, and find her way—one imperfect step at a time.

www.ingramcontent.com/pod-product-compliance
Lightning Source LLC
Chambersburg PA
CBHW051316130726
47987CB00004B/1828